J
Bio
Mao
2004

DATE DUE

APR 2 6 2005		
OCT 0 9 2007		
GAYLORD		PRINTED IN U.S.A.

D1124318

THE CHINESE REVOLUTION
and Mao Zedong in World History

Ann Malaspina

Enslow Publishers, Inc.

40 Industrial Road   PO Box 38
Box 398   Aldershot
Berkeley Heights, NJ 07922   Hants GU12 6BP
USA   UK

http://www.enslow.com

Library of Congress Cataloging-in-Publication Data

Malaspina, Ann, 1957–
    The Chinese revolution and Mao Zedong in world history / Ann
Malaspina.
        v. cm. — (In world history)
    Includes bibliographical references and index.
    Contents: Climbing Jiajin Mountain — The birth of a rebel — The end
of an empire — The barrel of the gun — The march to a new China —
A people rises up — Trouble and turmoil — The Cultural Revolution —
Opening the doors — Mao's legacy.
        ISBN 0-7660-1935-7
        1. Mao, Zedong, 1893–1976—Juvenile literature. 2. Communism—
China—History—Juvenile literature. 3. China—Politics and
government—20th century—Juvenile literature. [1. Mao, Zedong,
1893–1976. 2. Communism—China—History. 3. China—Politics and
government—20th century. 4. China—History—20th century.] I. Title.
II. Series.
    DS778.M3M235   2003
    951.05'092—dc21

                                                    2002156647

10 9 8 7 6 5 4 3 2 1

To Our Readers: We have done our best to make sure all Internet Addresses in
this book were active and appropriate when we went to press. However, the
author and the publisher have no control over and assume no liability for the
material available on those Internet sites or on other Web sites they may link to.
Any comments or suggestions can be sent by e-mail to comments@enslow.com or
to the address on the back cover.

Illustration Credits: Enslow Publishers, Inc., p. 4; Hulton Archive by
Getty Images, pp. 7, 14, 45, 49, 68, 82, 90, 107, 110; Reproduced from the
Collections of the Library of Congress, pp. 10, 19, 23, 25, 33, 37, 54, 59,
85, 95, 98.

Cover Illustration: Enslow Publishers, Inc. (Background); Reproduced
from the Collections of the Library of Congress (Mao Portrait).

Contents

Key events of Mao Zedong's revolution occurred in many Chinese provinces and cities. The Long March went through Sichuan. Above, is a current map of China.

Chapter 1

Climbing Jiajin Mountain

A line of soldiers climbed a trail up the snowy fields of Jiajin Mountain in the Sichuan Province of China in June 1935. The peasants in the region called the towering peak, Fairy Mountain. They believed it was magical. The wind blew so cold that some people claimed the snow on the mountain had not melted for a thousand years.

Since it was summer in the valleys, the soldiers wore thin cotton clothing and sandals. Some were barefoot. The lucky ones wrapped themselves in fur they had stolen from Tibetan horsemen. The soldiers carried guns and supplies on their backs. The army cooks bent under the weight of packs filled with big bags of rice. However, there was little water to boil for meals, and the air was too thin to light fires.

Behind the ragged soldiers in the First Army Unit of the Communist Red Army lay an eight-month journey across the heart of China. Before the soldiers lay a dream of what China might become if they were victorious. They wanted a country where the lines between the rich and the poor were erased, and private ownership was abolished. They dreamed of a country where peasants farmed their own land, and everyone had enough to eat. None was more determined than the unit's leader, a tall man with many new ideas, Mao Zedong (also spelled Mao Tse-tung).

China was in the grips of a bloody civil war. The Communists had been battling the ruling Guomindang, or Nationalists, since 1927. Poorly equipped and disorganized, the Red Army was losing badly. In the fall of 1934, the Guomindang army, led by General Chiang Kai-shek, surrounded the Communist stronghold in the southern province of Jiangxi. Desperate to escape, the revolutionaries began marching, first to the west, then turning north. Some eighty-six thousand Communist soldiers and supporters set forth on the Long March in October 1934.

Now the First Army Unit was facing its newest challenge. Jiajin Mountain rose before them. Mao, forty-one, had little choice but to go forward. To go west would require confronting hostile Tibetan warriors. Guomindang soldiers were gathered to the east. The only safe route to reach another Red Army unit, waiting with support, was to climb the mountain.

This scene from a Chinese tapestry depicts the Long March. It shows the harsh conditions experienced by the Red Army.

Many of Mao's soldiers had never seen snow. They wrapped their eyes in cloth to avoid snow blindness. They were told not to stop, or they would risk frostbite. The path disappeared after awhile, and some soldiers fell into icy gullies. Men slipped and shattered bones. Small avalanches spewed rocks and ice. Some who were already weak or ill did not survive. "We lost many good people. The weather was cold. Men froze to death. Some simply could not breathe,"[1] one marcher told writer Harrison E. Salisbury.

Most of the soldiers did survive Jiajin Mountain. Soon after, they met the Fourth Front Army in a small village. There, around ten thousand people celebrated and feasted on food stolen from landlords. They paused to listen to Mao, who urged the soldiers to stay united and strong to fight the Japanese Army. The Japanese were gaining strength in China's north. There was little time to rest. More peaks in the Great Snowy Mountain range awaited. Before the Long March was over, the Red Army would cross six thousand miles of China's wildest land. Many would die. One China expert called the march a "nightmare of death and pain."[2]

Despite the heavy losses, the Long March would prove a victory for Mao and the Chinese Communist party. But a long struggle still lay ahead for Mao and the rebel solders.

Chapter 2

Birth of a Rebel

The discontent of the Chinese people had been simmering for decades before the Long March. China had been a great nation, with a rich culture and an advanced civilization. By the late 1800s, China was in sharp decline. Corruption and weak leaders were crippling the Qing dynasty, which had ruled China since 1644. Western countries were exploiting China's resources. Most of the Chinese people were rural peasants. They had no land to call their own and little say in their own lives.

China in the 1890s

Mao Zedong grew up during this time of uncertainty. He was born on December 26, 1893, in Hunan, a large province of fertile hills and valleys in south-central China. Tea plantations, bamboo groves, and rice fields

Mao Zedong

spread across Hunan. Mao's family lived in the remote farming village of Shaoshan. As one writer noted, in Mao's day, no roads led to Shaoshan, only stony paths.

Daily life in Shaoshan had not changed much in hundreds of years. World events and politics seemed far away, while family relationships were most important. Chinese peasants depended on good harvests. When droughts came, they could not pay the high rent and taxes due to the landlords. Famines frequently swept through rural villages.

The Mao family relied on the rice harvest. However, they were fortunate to own land, instead of rent it from a landlord. Mao grew up in a comfortable farmhouse with a courtyard and tiled roof. Following the Chinese tradition, Mao was his family name and Zedong was the name given to him by his parents. His father and mother, Mao Rensheng and Wen Qimei, had seven children—two daughters and five sons—but only three boys survived childhood. Zedong's brothers, Mao Zemin and Mao Zetan, would join the Communist revolution. Later, the family adopted a girl named Mao Zehong.

Zedong, the eldest child, was very fond and respectful of his mother. Wen Qimei was a devout Buddhist with a gentle, tolerant nature. Although her husband was a "skeptic" and did not follow any religion, she gave her children religious instruction.

His mother, like most Chinese at the time, was illiterate. She wanted more for her sons. Zedong went to work in the fields when he was just six years old. Two

Source Document

My mother was a kind woman, generous and sympathetic, and ever ready to share what she had. She pitied the poor and often gave them rice when they came to ask for it during famines. But she could not do so when my father was present. He disapproved of charity. We had many quarrels in my home over this question.[1]

Mao Zedong particularly admired his mother's sympathy for peasants poorer than the Mao family.

years later, he was enrolled in the primary school in Shaoshan. There, Zedong learned to read and write Chinese. This was a challenge since Chinese writing uses fifty thousand characters, rather than twenty-six letters. Each character represents a word. A person needs to know about two thousand characters in order to read Chinese comfortably. Zedong's success in learning to read and write would set him apart from the majority of Chinese.

Confucianism

Zedong also studied the Chinese classics, or the ancient texts on Chinese government and culture, required by the schools. He read works by the great Chinese philosophers, including Confucius. The teachings of Confucius, who died in 479 B.C., formed the basis for Chinese culture and behavior for centuries. Confucius taught that families and societies should be organized based on rules of behavior. He considered benevolence the most important virtue. He also valued loyalty, courage, wisdom, and trustworthiness. Confucius felt that a nation's ruler should be like the father of a family. The ruler should set a good moral example for the people.

Mao also learned about legalism, a political philosophy founded by Han Fei, a rival of Confucius. In contrast to Confucianism, legalism relies on the absolute, or total, power of the state. Human beings are considered selfish. Social order is preserved with strict laws and discipline. The ruler is all-powerful. Laws are tools to keep the people under control. Legalism became the form of rulership for some Chinese emperors, giving them absolute power. Those who disobeyed the emperor were severely punished.

Like many of his classmates, Zedong preferred fiction to the Chinese classics. He liked the romantic stories of Old China. These tales of heroes and revolts left a strong impression of the glory won by rebels. Zedong also found he had a talent for writing. He would become a prolific writer and poet.

Chinese philosopher Confucius lived from 551 to 479 B.C. Mao disagreed with the ideas of Confucius, preferring those of Han Fei who founded the political philosophy called legalism.

Rebellious Spirit

Zedong's rebellious spirit was soon apparent. His teacher at the village school was strict and often beat the students. Unhappy at his treatment, one day when he was just ten years old, Zedong ran away from school, and his home. He wandered lost for three days before returning home. To his surprise, his teacher seemed to treat him with more respect afterward. "The result of my act of protest impressed me very much. It was a successful 'strike,'"[2] he said later.

Mao's father expected his eldest son would one day inherit the farm. When Zedong was thirteen, Mao Rensheng took him out of school. Zedong was to work the fields and keep the farm's business records. Zedong did not get along with his father. Mao Rensheng had a strong temper. He was impatient with his restless, curious son. The two often fought and disagreed. Later, Zedong would criticize his father for being unsympathetic toward peasants.

Zedong was determined to resume his education. He managed to escape his chores in 1910 and hire two tutors in a nearby town. One of his tutors gave him a pamphlet called "The Dismemberment of China." It discussed how nations such as Japan and France had colonized Asia and dominated China.

China's Early History

During his studies, Mao learned about China's great history. The Chinese call their country *Zhongguo*, which means "central land or the Middle Kingdom."

The name reflects their belief that China is the center of the world and the only true civilization. In fact, Chinese have shared a common culture for longer than most other peoples. The Chinese have made important contributions to the world, including the art of papermaking, tea, gunpowder, silk cloth, and the compass.

The Chinese Empire was founded in 221 B.C. when a prince from the western state of Qin united seven warring states. Shi Huang Ti, meaning "First Emperor," formed the Qin Empire, the first of many Chinese dynasties, or ruling families. He standardized writing, currency, and weights and measures. He established a government that built roads and palaces. However, Shi Huang Ti was a cruel ruler. He adopted the philosophy of legalism, rejecting the benevolent Confucian ideals. He persecuted the rich, burned books, and killed scholars. Dissent was not tolerated. Small crimes were punished by the loss of a hand or foot. He forced prisoners to build the Great Wall of China to keep out barbarians from the north. Mao came to admire the First Emperor after studying about him.

The Qin dynasty lasted only fourteen years. Rebellions by peasants and ministers ended the use of legalism as a state philosophy. The Qin dynasty was replaced by the more friendly Han dynasty. More empires followed. In 1644, Manchus from the northeast established the Qing dynasty. The Qing dynasty led China during three centuries of prosperity, stability, and expansion, but those good years soon came to an end.

Foreign Exploitation

China became isolated during the Qing dynasty. It fell behind the modernization and industrialization occurring in Western countries. When its isolation ended, new problems arose. By the mid-1800s, Europeans had discovered China's riches. They came to trade in China's tea, silk, porcelain, and other products. To balance the trade, they sold opium, an addictive drug, to the Chinese. The Qing emperor banned the opium trade in 1800, but the foreigners ignored the ban. After the Chinese seized twenty thousand chests of British opium in Guangzhou, the British went on the attack.

The Opium War raged from 1839 to 1842. China was defeated and forced to establish seaports to receive foreign goods, such as imports of cheap cloth, which further damaged local economies. China also had to give the island of Hong Kong to Great Britain. As a British colony, Hong Kong became an important trade center. Under the terms of a ninety-nine-year lease, Hong Kong was not returned to China until 1997.

Japan also posed a threat to China. The two countries were long rivals. Japan defeated China in the Sino-Japanese War of 1894 to 1895. Japan forced China to give up control of and to hand over Taiwan and other lands. Gradually, other countries dominated China, as well. Japanese and other foreigners were allowed to open factories in China. Germany, Britain, Russia, and France demanded that China hand over land. The foreign powers divided China into "spheres of influence," each dominated by one nation. Unable to resist, China fell into serious debt. The government raised taxes, making the Chinese people poor.

The imperial government did little to protect China. By this time, the Qing dynasty had become corrupt. To add to its difficulties, by 1850, China's population had grown to over 400 million people. China was the world's most populous country. This led to a shortage of jobs and low pay. The ordinary worker had a harder time making a living. Peasants had smaller farms to raise their food. Farmers overused their land, causing soil erosion. "Too many people trying to make a living on too few resources naturally also exacerbated social tensions,"[3] wrote Patricia Buckley Ebrey, in the *Cambridge Illustrated History of China*.

The Boxer Rebellion

In 1898, radical reformers urged the emperor, Guangxu, to modernize China and to change the structure of government and society. The emperor began issuing proclamations to bring change, but he had little influence. His aunt, the Empress Dowager Cixi, held the reigns of power, and she was against the reforms. She executed many of the radicals, putting a temporary stop to the movement for change.

Unrest swept through China in 1899 and 1900. A secret society of peasants from the north organized to oppose Western imperialism. The society was called the "Righteous and Harmonious Fists"; the Europeans called them the Boxers because of their martial arts skills. The Boxers wanted to expel foreigners and foreign influence from China. They resented the missionaries who were converting the Chinese to Christianity.

Supported by the empress and the government, the Boxers burned down churches and houses of Westerners, and killed Chinese Christians. By June 1900, the Boxers occupied Beijing and Tianjin. The

During the Boxer Rebellion, armed peasants in the 11th Regiment of infantry stormed the walls of Tientsin, China.

Western countries fought back. In August 1900, a coalition of British, French, Russian, American, German, and Japanese soldiers fought their way into Beijing. The troops, numbering nearly twenty thousand, defeated the Boxers, and the empress fled the city. To settle the conflict, China had to pay heavy fines, sign treaties favoring the foreign countries, and allow foreign troops into Beijing. The foreigners saw China as a barbaric country. The Boxer Rebellion's bitter aftermath fueled frustration among the Chinese people. More than ever, they wanted China's independence.

Awakening

Zedong was aware of injustices close to home. When he was young, a famine devastated Changsha, the provincial capital, and thousands were starving. "The starving sent a delegation to the civil governor to beg for relief, but he replied to them haughtily, 'Why haven't you food? There is plenty in the city. I always have enough,'" Mao recalled later. The people organized a demonstration and drove out the governor. A new governor arrested the rebel leaders. Many protestors were beheaded and their heads were displayed in public. "I never forgot it. I felt that there with the rebels were ordinary people like my own family and I deeply resented the injustice of the treatment given to them," said Mao.[4]

In 1910, Zedong enrolled in a school in a nearby market town, Xiangxiang. The school offered classes in science and Western ideas. For the first time, Zedong learned about world events. Eager to see what lay beyond his home, Zedong enrolled in a school in Changsha. He was seventeen when he is said to have walked thirty miles to Changsha. In Changsha, Zedong began exploring ideas that would later develop into his political philosophy.

While Zedong's life led him far from Shaoshan, he never forgot his early years. "It was there that Mao had hammered out his own revolutionary philosophy, a philosophy steeped in knowledge of the Chinese peasant and the countryside," wrote Harrison E. Salisbury.[5] Mao's sympathy with the hard, simple life of the Chinese peasant would form the basis of his political ideas. (Much later, his bodyguards would use the nickname "the Old Peasant" to refer to Mao.) Discontent and new ideas were sweeping across China, and Mao was taken by the tide.

End of an Empire

The failure of the Boxer Rebellion was a hard lesson for China. The imperial government saw that China had become very weak. As the twentieth century began, the Qing dynasty launched reforms to strengthen its military, develop trade and industry, and regain control over the provinces. Yet China's government could not save itself. The Chinese people no longer wanted to be ruled by emperors in Beijing. They wanted a new government, one that was responsive to the people's needs and open to progress.

Uprising

The movement for a republican government, or a government run by the people, found a spokesman in Sun Yat-sen. Sun was a doctor who had spent much of his life outside China. He was born in 1866 to a farming

The Chinese revolutionary Sun Yat-sen led the uprising against the Qing dynasty and the creation of the Chinese republic in 1912.

family in southeast China. He studied in missionary schools in Honolulu, Hawaii. He later went to Hong Kong, where he trained as a physician. Sun also converted to Christianity. He practiced medicine only briefly for he was more interested in shaping China's future. Like other revolutionaries of his time, Sun wanted to free China of foreign control and overthrow the Qing dynasty.

After he returned to China, in the mid-1890s, Sun led an unsuccessful revolt against the imperial government. Sun was a skilled leader who drew many people together behind the common goal of ending China's imperial rule. In 1905, while in exile in Japan, Sun founded the United League, China's first modern revolutionary organization. Most members of the group were Chinese living overseas.

Sun's political theory included the "Three People's Principles," a combination of nationalism, democracy, and socialism. Nationalism is a philosophy in which a person's loyalty is to the nation; one's nation is considered superior to other nations. In a democracy, the government is run by and for the people. Socialism is a system in which the means of production is shared by everyone in common ownership; everyone has an equal share in the goods produced, even though each person may not produce the same amount of goods. Sun thought China had to go through stages to reach a democracy. He also sought a strong central government to protect China from exploitation.

The 1911 Revolution

It took years of struggle by Sun and other republican revolutionaries to topple the Qing dynasty. Many uprisings failed. Meanwhile, the empire grew weaker. In 1908, the Qing Empress Dowager Cixi and Emperor Guangxu both died within days of each other. The last Chinese emperor, Pu Yi, a three-year-old boy, ascended the throne.

Sun Yat-sen was in the United States, gathering support for his revolution, when an anti-Manchu organization of Chinese troops rose on October 10, 1911.

Members of the Imperial Chinese Army pose on October 16, 1911, the day before they rose up against the Manchus.

The rebels took over Wuhan, an industrial center on the Middle Yangtze River. Overpowered, the Manchus were defeated. On January 1, 1912, Sun was inaugurated as provisional president of the Republic of China in the city of Nanjing. Yet Sun lacked the power and foreign support to unify China. He handed the presidency to Yuan Shikai, a military leader in northern China.

The Qing Empire officially came to an end on February 12, 1912, when the emperor Pu Yi gave up his title. Just seven years old, Pu Yi was allowed to live on in the Imperial City in Beijing. In 1924, a warlord expelled him from the palace and he took refuge with the Japanese. In 1934, he was given the title of emperor of Manchuria by the occupying Japanese army and ruled until 1945.

The Guomindang

Yuan Shikai, president of China in 1912, quickly proved no better than an emperor. He used the military to gain power for himself. Soon he was a dictator. Outraged, Sun Yat-sen and others organized a new political party. Founded in 1912, the Guomindang, or the National People's party, sought to unite China and provide economic security for the people. The Guomindang won the majority in national parliamentary elections in the next years. Yuan suppressed the Guomindang, and Sun fled to Japan, but the party still gained support in parts of China.

China's condition soon worsened. After Yuan's death in 1916, China broke up into warring regions. The regions were led by warlords, or military leaders who used violent force to control their kingdoms. The warlord era was a period of violence, oppression, and disunity. Military strength replaced political authority. The peasants paid high taxes to support the warlords. China fell into more foreign debt. It was on this canvas that China's youth and intellectuals painted a revolution of new ideas.

May Fourth Movement

The revolution of ideas was sparked, in part, by events outside China. During Yuan's rule, World War I broke out in June 1914. The war began when an assassin gunned down Archduke Franz Ferdinand of Austria-Hungary in Sarajevo, the capital of Austria-Hungary's province of Bosnia-Herzegovina. During WWI, which lasted from 1914 to 1918, China joined the Allies—which included the United States, France, and Great Britain—against Germany. Chinese soldiers did not go to battle, but thousands of Chinese laborers worked in France behind the lines. The Allies defeated Germany.

At the war's end, China expected to recover its land from foreign occupiers. This included Shandong, a coastal Chinese province controlled by Germany. Unexpectedly, during the Paris Peace Conference, the Allies gave Shandong to Japan. The Chinese felt betrayed. This event added to growing discontent among young people.

The discontent grew into a movement for change. On May 4, 1919, three thousand college students marched into Tiananmen Square in Beijing to protest China's treatment by the Allies. The students and intellectuals called on China to embrace progress, democracy, and science. They urged China to move away from its old ways. This was called the May Fourth Movement.

Mao's Education

Like many young men, Mao Zedong joined Sun Yat-sen's Republican army in 1911. He spent six months in the army, but he never saw combat. Instead, he stayed on duty in the army garrison in Changsha. He wrote letters for men in his squad. "I could write, I knew something about books, and they respected my 'great learning,'" recalled Mao.[1]

After the Qing dynasty collapsed, Mao returned to his studies. In 1912, he enrolled in a traditional school in Changsha, where he read Chinese history. He soon left to study alone in the local library. There, he discovered Western classics such as Adam Smith's *The Wealth of Nations*, Darwin's *On the Origin of Species*, and Herbert Spencer's *Logic*. He also read the work of Western political philosophers.

In 1913, Mao enrolled in the Hunan First Normal School, where his teacher, Yang Changji, became an important influence. Yang advocated combining

Western science with Chinese culture. "He taught ethics, he was an idealist and a man of high moral character. He believed in his ethics very strongly and tried to imbue his students with the desire to become just, moral, virtuous men, useful in society," Mao said.[2]

New Ideas

Mao was sympathetic to the May Fourth Movement. He joined discussion groups and wrote for magazines devoted to new ideas. In 1915, a magazine, *New Youth*, was founded by Chen Duxiu, the radical intellectual who led the May Fourth Movement. Mao's first article in *New Youth* described a personal fitness program for Chinese to follow in order to become military heroes. In other articles, Mao criticized Confucianism. He urged people to rise up against old traditions. "We are awakened! The world is ours, the nation is ours, society is ours. If we do not speak, who will speak? If we do not act, who will act? If we do not rise up and fight, who will rise up and fight?" he wrote in 1919.[3]

After graduating from teachers' college in 1918, Mao moved to Beijing. He took a clerical job at the Beijing University library. The head librarian, Li Dazhao, became Mao's mentor, or teacher. Mao returned to Changsha in 1919 and became involved in political activity supporting the May Fourth Movement. He got students to protest the Allied leaders and boycott Japanese goods. He also published *New Hunan*, a magazine that supported the May

Fourth Movement. After the governor banned the magazine, Mao led protestors to Beijing to demand that the governor be removed from office.

In 1920, Mao married Yang Kaihui, the daughter of his teacher, Yang Changji. Mao had been married as a young teenager. His father had arranged a union between Zedong and a local village girl, but Mao did not recognize that first arranged marriage. Yang and Mao had three sons: Mao Anying, Mao Anqing, and Mao Anlong.

Communism

Mao began to read about communism, a political philosophy attracting interest among Chinese intellectuals. Communism is based on the ideas of Karl Marx and Friedrich Engels. In 1848, the two German philosophers published *The Communist Manifesto*. They wrote about transforming society by abolishing social classes. The major resources and means of production would be owned by the state. Private property would not exist. In theory, everybody would share all work, according to their abilities, and everybody would benefit, according to their needs. The state would be responsible for taking care of the people. Communism would create a more just and equal society. Marx and Engels predicted it would liberate the members of the proletariat, or working class, who work for low pay in the factories of Europe.

Mao read many books about communism. These books "especially deeply carved my mind, and built up

Source Document

What is Communism? Communism is the doctrine of the conditions of the liberation of the proletariat. What is the proletariat? The proletariat is that class in society which lives entirely from the sale of its labor and does not draw profit from any kind of capital; whose weal and woe, whose life and death, whose sole existence depends on the demand for labor—hence, on the changing state of business, on the vagaries of unbridled competition. The proletariat, or the class of proletarians, is, in a word, the working class of the 19th Century.[4]

Friedrich Engels explained the theory of communism in his 1847 book The Principles of Communism.

in me a faith in Marxism, from which . . . I did not afterwards waver," he told Edgar Snow. "By the summer of 1920 I had become, in theory and to some extent in action, a Marxist, and from this time on I considered myself a Marxist."[5]

Russian Revolution

By 1920, communism had already toppled the tsars of Russia. The tsars were similar to the Chinese emperors.

For many centuries, Russia had been led by tsarist regimes. While living in luxury, the tsars allowed their people little freedom or the means to escape from poverty. Many Russians felt that communism was a better alternative. Russian Communists overthrew Tsar Nicholas II in the October Revolution of 1917 and seized power. The revolutionaries, known as Bolsheviks, were led by Vladimir Ilich Lenin, the founder of the Communist party in Russia.

A brilliant intellectual, trained as a lawyer, Lenin suffered under the tsarist regime. He was exiled for revolutionary activity. Lenin was determined to bring change to Russia. He transformed Marx's ideas into a political revolution. Marx thought that workers and peasants would carry out the revolution on their own. Lenin maintained that a small group of leaders should lead the revolution. He often called it "the dictatorship of the proletariat," which meant the Bolshevik party would impose its doctrines on all of Russia. Later, China would adopt Lenin's idea of rule by a select few.

Lenin set up a dictatorship, using terror and force to carry out his vision. He routed out his enemies with a secret police force. He even imposed artificial famines to erase opposition. Lenin "waged war on the intelligentsia and on religious believers, wiping out any traces of civil liberty and a free press," wrote David Remnick in *Time* magazine.[6] In other words, Lenin would not allow criticism.

European Communist thinkers and leaders had a very large influence on Mao Zedong. However, Mao knew that he needed to develop a form of communism that would work for the Chinese people. Pictured on the flag behind Mao are, from left to right: Josef Stalin, Vladimir Lenin, Friedrich Engels, and Karl Marx.

Chinese Communist Party

In 1921, a group of scholars secretly organized the Chinese Communist party in Shanghai. Mao's mentor Li Dazhao, along with Chen Duxiu, were the two founding fathers. On July 21, 1921, Mao, at the age of twenty-seven, led the Hunan delegation to the First Congress of the Chinese Communist party in Shanghai. At this first meeting of the Chinese

Communist party, Mao was named secretary of the Hunan branch of the party. Advisors from Comintern, or Communist International, a group that spread communism beyond Russia's borders, helped advise the party.

China and Russia shared an important feature. The peasants and workers in Russia and China had labored for centuries under tsars and emperors, respectively. In China, the warlord era left the peasants worse off than ever. Communism held out the promise that people would share in the nation's wealth and avoid starvation.

Chapter 4

The Barrel of the Gun

For China to move forward, the warlords had to be defeated and the country had to be united. The Soviet Union, which was the new name taken by Russia in 1922, urged the Chinese Communist party to join with the Guomindang, which had been gaining strength in many provinces. Together, the two groups would have a better chance of overturning the warlords and bringing the country together under a republican government. In 1923, Sun Yat-sen agreed to form the United Front between the Chinese Communist party and the Guomindang.

Chiang Kia-shek

For a few years, the two groups joined forces against the warlords, but cooperation ended after Sun died in 1925. Chiang Kai-shek, his colleague, took his place as the leader of the Guomindang. Chiang was an experienced military commander, as well as a skillful politician.

Like Mao, Chiang rose from modest beginnings. He was born on October 31, 1887, in Fenghua, a remote farming village in Zhejiang, the eastern province of China. His father earned a living as a salt seller. Yet Chiang never shared Mao's sympathy with China's peasants. He was more interested in building power bases in China's cities. He wanted to establish China as a world power.

Chiang left China to train at a military academy in Tokyo, Japan, in 1907, where he met Sun Yat-sen. Chiang returned to China in 1911 to join Sun in the overthrow of the imperial government. Chiang received military training in Moscow. He was then named commandant of the Whampoa Military Academy, the training center for Guomindang soldiers. Chiang became commander in chief of the Nationalist Army, known as the White Army. After Sun's death, Chiang was the natural choice to lead the party.

Northern Expedition

Chiang's military prowess offered new hope in the unification of China. In 1926, with Communist support, Chiang embarked on the Northern Expedition to fight the warlords. At that time, the Guomindang controlled only two provinces. To divert attention, Communist rebels incited strikes and upheaval in southeastern China. By March 1927, the Guomindang

Mao Zedong and Chiang Kai-shek (pictured) would become arch enemies in the struggle for power in China.

armies had pushed back the warlords and taken all of southeastern China.

Unlike Sun Yat-sen, Chiang was not willing to share his revolution with the Communists. He was convinced they were disruptive and posed a threat to his authority. By 1927, Chiang had decided that the Communists were enemies, rather than friends. Chiang set out to destroy the Communist strongholds.

At dawn on April 12, 1927, Guomindang troops surrounded Communist-held areas in Shanghai, the port city on the East China Sea. Shanghai was a crowded and bustling trading center. Half the city was dominated by foreigners and foreign businesses. The Chinese side of Shanghai was poor and working-class. Many Chinese workers were members of unions and sympathetic to the Communists.

The White Army of the Guomindang staged its attack in the working-class areas. Taken by surprise, some four hundred Communist sympathizers were killed. Zhou Enlai, the top Communist party official in Shanghai, ordered a general strike of workers the next day. Then about one thousand workers, including women and children who worked in the textile mills, marched to the military headquarters to hand in a petition about the strike. Guomindang soldiers fired on the unarmed protestors. Many were killed, and more were wounded. Thousands of Communists were killed in what is known as the "White Terror."

In other provinces, the Guomindang were capturing and executing Communists. In May 1927, fighting erupted in Changsha. An estimated ten thousand people died. Communists and even suspected Communists were executed by the Guomindang. In another province, Hubei, thousands of villagers were slaughtered.

China's Peasants

Like many Communists, Mao cooperated for a time with the Guomindang. He held important positions in the governing committee of the party. As relations between the two groups broke down, Mao was removed from those positions. Meanwhile, he was busy organizing peasants in Hunan, his home province.

Life was a struggle for China's peasants, who comprised about 80 percent of the population. Droughts, floods, and famine were common. They paid high taxes and saw little profit from their hard work. Mao sought to harness their dissatisfaction.

Mao wanted, not just to improve the peasants' lives, but to gain their loyalty in a Communist revolution. In 1926, Mao researched peasants living near Changsha. In his historic document, "Report on an Investigation of the Peasant Movement in Hunan," Mao stated that peasants would be a major force in a revolution. He also described his vision of a revolution. "A revolution is not a dinner party, or writing an essay, or painting a picture, or doing embroidery; it cannot be so refined, so leisurely and gentle, so temperate, kind, courteous, restrained and magnanimous.

Source Document

In a very short time, in China's central, southern and northern provinces, several hundred million peasants will rise like a mighty storm, like a hurricane, a force so swift and violent that no power, however great, will be able to hold it back. They will smash all the trammels that bind them and rush forward along the road to liberation. They will sweep all the imperialists, warlords, corrupt officials, local tyrants and evil gentry into their graves. Every revolutionary party and every revolutionary comrade will be put to the test, to be accepted or rejected as they decide. There are three alternatives. To march at their head and lead them? To trail behind them, gesticulating and criticizing? Or to stand in their way and oppose them? Every Chinese is free to choose, but events will force you to make the choice quickly. [1]

This quote from Mao's "Report on an Investigation of the Peasant Movement in Hunan" shows that Mao saw great power in the large peasant class of China.

A revolution is an insurrection, an act of violence by which one class overthrows another," wrote Mao.[2]

Despite Mao's efforts, peasant support of the Communists was dwindling. Many had been killed. Others were afraid of opposing Chiang's army. Humiliated by many defeats, on August 1, 1927, the Communist leader Zhou Enlai ordered Communists to rise up against the Guomindang in Nanchang. The Communists won a victory with few shots fired. The Nanchang Uprising is celebrated as the establishment of the Communist's Red Army. Mao realized that a strong army was necessary to achieve political ideals. "From now on, we should pay the greatest attention to military affairs. We must know that political power is obtained from the barrel of the gun," Mao wrote in August 1927.[3]

Nationalists Triumph

Still, the Communists could not defeat the Guomindang. In the fall of 1927, Mao helped organize an unsuccessful uprising in Changsha. The Autumn Harvest Uprising, as it was known, was a disaster for the Communists and Mao. Mao was expelled from the central committee of the Communist party. The Communists retreated to the countryside. By year's end, party membership had fallen drastically. In 1928, Chiang's troops captured Beijing.

For now, the Communists were defeated. The Guomindang had overwhelmed the warlords, crushed the Communists, and reunited the country. The national government was moved to Nanjing. From 1928 to 1937, the Guomindang controlled much of China. They made some reforms, but the lives of the peasants did not improve much. With a stronger leadership, China began regaining its autonomy, or independence. Some Western countries pulled out of China, and foreign countries recognized Chiang Kai-shek's government.

Jiangxi Soviet

Mao and the Red Army soldiers were forced to flee to the countryside. Mao settled in the mountains of south China where he established the Jiangxi Soviet. He created a Soviet-style government and built up the Red Army. Rather than capturing cities, as the Soviet advisers urged, Mao focused on gaining peasant support. Mao took land from landlords and gave it to the peasants. In doing so, he won over more peasants. By 1930, Mao was acting independently from the Soviet-dominated Communist party. In three years, the Jiangxi Soviet grew rapidly; the Red Army grew, as well.

Mao had an able assistant, Zhu De. Zhu was a talented military leader. He had been a warlord in the 1920s and an opium addict. But he fought his opium addiction and put aside his wealth to join the Communist party. Zhu was skilled at the art of war and a natural leader. The men who followed Zhu into battle adored him. Zhu often went without shoes to share hardships with his men.

The Red Army

Zhu led an army of volunteer soldiers from across China. Some were as young as fourteen years old. Many were farm laborers and craftsmen. Only a few were merchants and intellectuals. They were paid by income from their land or public land taken from landlords. As journalist Edgar Snow wrote, "I soon discovered that the great mass of the Red soldiery was made up of young peasants and workers who believed themselves to be fighting for their homes, their land, and their country."[4] The Red Army officers were only in their mid-twenties. Some had graduated from military academies in the Soviet Union.

Under the officers' command, the army developed its unique fighting style. The army would build up

---

Source Document

The enemy advances, we retreat.

The enemy halts, we move in.

The enemy tires, we attack.

The enemy retreats, we pursue.[5]

Mao made the Red Army learn this four-line poem, made up of sixteen Chinese characters, which rhymes in the original Chinese.

peasant support in the countryside, then encircle cities and close in on the Guomindang. The army's meager supply of weapons was mostly captured from the enemy.

Without professional training, and lacking supplies and arms, the Red Army developed the tactics of guerrilla warfare. Instead of attacking head-on, they used knowledge of local terrain to ambush the enemy, then quickly retreat. Mao later wrote:

> When the invader pierces deep into the heart of the weaker country and occupies her territory in a cruel and oppressive manner, there is no doubt that conditions of terrain, climate, and society in general offer obstacles to his progress and may be used to advantage by those who oppose him. In guerrilla warfare we turn these advantages to the purpose of resisting and defeating the enemy. . .[6]

The Red Army set out to win the loyalty of the peasants. The soldiers were told to take nothing from them and to pay fairly for food and clothing. Thus, tens of thousands of peasants pledged their allegiance to the Communists. These tactics were encouraged by Mao. "Modern warfare is not a matter in which armies alone can determine victory or defeat. Especially in guerrilla combat, we must rely on the force of the popular masses, for it is only thus that we can have a guarantee of success," Mao wrote in 1937.[7]

Losing Ground
In 1930, Mao's Red Army captured Changsha, then withdrew. A second assault on Changsha was a disaster.

The Communists suffered heavy losses. In November 1930, two months after the failed attack, Mao's wife, Yang Kaihui, was beheaded on the orders of the governor. Their children were hidden by relatives and secretly sent to Shanghai. A few months later, the youngest, Anlong, died of a disease called dysentery. Guomindang soldiers dug up the graves of Mao's parents, according to one account. These attacks on Mao Zedong's family indicated that the Guomindang considered him one of its chief enemies.

Mao, dressed in the simple cap and uniform of the Red Army, speaks during a Communist rally in 1930.

Despite these tragedies, Mao was gaining strength as a leader. In 1931, the All-China Congress of Chinese Soviets elected Mao as chairman of the first All-China Soviet Government. Zhu De was elected as the military commander. (Mao would be reelected in 1934 at the Second All-China Soviet Congress.) However, a famine in northwest China from 1929 to 1931 had killed between 5 and 10 million people, adding to the hardships endured by China's peasants.

The Guomindang rule was never complete. Many areas lay beyond the reach of the nationalists. Still, by 1934, the White Army surrounded the Red Army in Jiangxi Province, the Communist stronghold. In a desperate flight for safety, Communists began to march, first west, and then turning to the north. The Communists needed to find a new base. They needed an area to call their own.

Chapter 5

The People Rise Up

The Communists moved to escape the Guomindang army. Mao and his new, pregnant wife, a revolutionary named He Zizhen, joined about eighty-six thousand Communist soldiers and supporters on October 18, 1934. The couple left their two-year-old son, Anhong, with Mao's brother, Mao Zetan, who was staying with the rearguard group. Zetan later had to leave the boy with a bodyguard. Mao Anhong was never seen by his parents again.

The Long March

The Red Army lugged weapons, food, maps, printing presses, and other heavy equipment. They marched single file over stone paths crossing hills and rice paddies. On their long retreat, the soldiers crossed rivers and scaled mountains, staying out of sight on the plains and roads. Mao and the other leaders stayed up nights to plan tactics for the next day.

The Communists met disaster in late November when they tried to cross the Xiang River in the north of Guangxi Province. The Red Army had to face both the White Army and the local warlord. They battled through barbed wire and concrete blockhouses. Outgunned by machine guns and artillery, the Red soldiers suffered heavy casualties. According to eye-witness accounts, the Xiang River flowed red with blood and bodies. During the week it took the Red Army to cross the river, the Communists lost fifty thousand men.

After this episode, the Red Army dropped some of its supplies in order to move faster. Yet they were unsure where they were headed. In January 1935, the battered guerrillas were able to seize the city of Zunyi in Guizhou Province. In Zunyi, Communist party leaders met in a major conference to discuss the war. During the meeting, Mao voiced criticisms of the military action as planned by the Soviet-backed party leadership.

Mao suggested that the army use unconventional guerrilla tactics. Zhou Enlai, a respected military commander, proposed that Mao take over army leadership. Zhou became one of Mao's most trusted subordinates for decades to come. Mao did not receive formal leadership of the Chinese Communist party until 1943, but he was now considered the leader of both the Communist party and the Red Army.

Mao Zedong (left) and Zhou Enlai take part in the Long March in 1935. The Long March took over a year and formed the survivors into a close knit group loyal to Mao.

North to Fight Japan

Mao decided the march should not be a retreat. Instead, it became a crusade north to fight the Japanese. The Japanese Army had invaded northern China in the early 1930s and was moving south. "March north to fight Japan!" became the slogan of the Long March. From then on, the army did not march in a straight line or in one body. Several columns would zigzag and backtrack to keep the White Army unsure of the Red Army's location. Not every Communist commander followed Mao. Some men broke off to establish their own bases.

Many obstacles lay ahead. Guomindang troops and local warlords prevented the Red Army from crossing the Yangtze River. So the Communists were unable to establish a base in Sichuan Province, as they had hoped. Instead, they were forced to turn south to escape. They then headed north, staying close to the Tibetan border. Their final destination was the northern province of Shaanxi.

The Red Army walked many miles every day. Cold, hunger, and disease killed many of the marchers. Without adequate food, they foraged for weeds and berries. They suffered from malnutrition, frostbite, and despair.

Luding Bridge

One of the Red Army's most daring feats occurred in May 1935. The Red Army needed to cross the Dadu River in Sichuan Province. There were not enough

Source Document

The Long March
(October 1935)

The Red Army fears not the trials of the Long March,
Holding light ten thousand crags and torrents.
The Five Ridges wind like gentle ripples,
And the majestic Wumeng roll by, globules of clay.
Warm the steep cliffs lapped by the waters of Jinsha,
Cold the iron chains spanning the Dadu River.
Min Mountain's thousand li* of snow joyously crossed,
The three Armies march on, each face glowing.[1]

*A li is a Chinese unit of measurement equal to 547 yards.

This poem, written by Mao Zedong, describes the triumph of capturing the Luding Bridge.

ferry boats where they needed to cross. One unit was ordered to go one hundred miles upstream to Luding. In Luding, a long narrow bridge, made of iron links and wooden planking, crossed the river. The bridge was controlled by Guomindang soldiers on the other side. "One by one Red soldiers stepped forward to risk their lives. . . . Hand grenades and Mausers [a type of rifle] were strapped to their backs, and soon they were swinging out above the boiling river, moving hand over hand, clinging to the iron chains," wrote Edgar Snow.[2] The Guomindang removed the wooden floor planks on one side. They fired at the Red Army, and set fire to the planks. The Red Army put out the fires. All but a few soldiers made it to the other shore.

Many miles lay ahead. The army climbed the icy peaks of the Great Snowy Mountains. Bombing raids by the Guomindang Air Force injured Mao's wife, He Zizhen, and others. Later, they crossed the treacherous grasslands. Men sank in the mud and sickened from eating raw vegetables.

In October 1935, Mao and his soldiers straggled into Wayaboa in Shaanxi Province, just south of the Great Wall. The Long March was over. Historians estimate that about eight thousand marchers reached Shaanxi Province, where they were joined by thousands of Communist soldiers and supporters. Many thousands had been lost, some dead and others injured or deserted, in the six-thousand-mile march. It hardly seemed a victory, yet by surviving the ordeal, the Communists gained hope that one day they would prevail in China. Importantly, the Long March established Mao as the Communist leader.

Mao's New Life

At first, Mao led the Communist movement from a cave in a hillside village, Bao'an. He was thin and gaunt, and his life was in upheaval. His brother, Mao Zetan, was killed in combat in 1935. Mao Zedong and his wife, He Zizhen, had lost two children: Their two-year-old son and a newborn daughter were left with peasant families and never seen again. He Zizhen was still recovering from shrapnel injuries. She soon gave birth to another girl, Li Min. But Mao's wife became unhappy. She decided to leave China for the Soviet Union to have the shrapnel removed. While being treated in the Soviet Union, she gave birth to a son, who died at the age of ten months.

With his wife gone, Mao fell in love with another woman. In 1939, Mao married Jiang Qing, a Shanghai actress twenty-one years younger than himself. Mao and Jiang Qing had a daughter, Li Na, who was born in 1940. Meanwhile, Mao made the transformation from revolutionary guerrilla to political leader.

Political Philosophy

The Communist leaders soon left the caves and moved to Yan'an, about sixty miles away. Yan'an was a market town where traders brought timber, salt, and other goods to sell. Above the town towered a white pagoda. It became a symbol for the young people who walked hundreds of miles to Yan'an to join the revolution. The Communist rebels went to work. Small industries were launched, and fields were planted.

Mao occupied a merchant's house on the slopes of a mountain. He spent his days and nights studying and writing. He was forming ideas about China's future. Mao wanted to free China from the grasp of foreign powers. He wanted a new system of government and a new social structure. Gradually, he developed a political

This picture of Mao and his fourth wife, Jiang Qing was taken in 1945, six years after they married.

philosophy known as Maoism. It was a combination of Marxism and socialistic thought, adapted to the people and conditions of China.

Marx had glorified industrial workers as the leaders of the Socialist revolution. In the Soviet Union, Lenin led a revolution in cities for the workers in factories and industries. In contrast, Mao sought to harness the support, and change the lives, of rural peasants. Mao also advocated the idea of perpetual, or continuous, revolution. By this, Mao meant that revolution was a process that was always occurring.

Mao believed in class struggle, or the conflict between the peasants and the wealthy. In Mao's view, every person was born into a class. "In class society everyone lives as a member of a particular class, and every kind of thinking, without exception, is stamped with the brand of a class," he wrote in 1937.[3] If a person's grandfather was a landlord, then he or she belonged to the landlord class, even if the land was lost. Mao considered landlords and other members of the wealthy class bad. They had oppressed the peasants for too long. It was time for the peasants to rise up.

Mao wrote long essays about his ideas. Followers of Mao carried copies of the essays in their pockets. They studied his words, day and night, memorizing every phrase. More and more people were drawn to his ideas.

In Yan'an, Mao built his political power to ensure that he would be the man to lead China. He surrounded himself with trusted friends such as Deng

Source Document

Not only do we want to change a China that is politically oppressed and economically exploited into a China that is politically free and economically prosperous, we also want to change the China which is being kept ignorant and backward under the sway of the old culture into an enlightened and progressive China under the sway of a new culture. In short, we want to build a new China. Our aim in the cultural sphere is to build a new Chinese national culture.[4]

Mao's essay, "On New Democracy," appeared in Chinese Culture *magazine in 1940.*

Xiaoping, Lin Biao, and other loyal Communists. Some of his comrades began rewriting the history of China to make Mao the center of it. It was a hint of the godlike role to which Mao aspired. Mao also began to punish people whose loyalty to communism was in doubt. Thousands of people were persecuted for betraying the ideas of the Communist party.

Fighting the Gray Dragon

Meanwhile, Japanese aggression cast a darkening shadow. Japan was interested in the northern Chinese province of Manchuria, which was rich in minerals and other natural resources. A bomb of unknown origin blew up the Japanese railway near Shenyang, Manchuria, in September 1931. The Japanese Army used the incident to justify occupying southern Manchuria. By February 1932, the Japanese Army occupied all of Manchuria. Japan proclaimed it the state of Manchukuo. Japanese soldiers and settlers took over businesses and moved into private homes.

As the Communists built strength in Shaanxi, the Japanese Army was moving south. The Communists could not fight the Japanese on their own. They felt the Guomindang government was not doing enough to stop the Japanese. Even the Guomindang soldiers perceived the danger of losing to Japan. In December 1936, one of Chiang Kai-shek's generals kidnapped him. As a condition of his release, he agreed to join with the Communists. Thus, the Guomindang and the Communists formed the United Front against Japan. Still, the two never trusted each other. Fighting continued to erupt between them. Mao's brother, Mao Zemin, who had made the Long March, was killed in 1942, in an anti-Communist purge in Sinkiang.

A full-scale war between China and Japan broke out in 1937. The Japanese Army set out to conquer cities, roads, and railroads. The Chinese Army, under Chiang, was unable to protect its cities. The Japanese Army took Beijing and Tianjin, then the trading port of Shanghai and Nanjing, the national capital. In late 1938, Hankou and Guiangzhou also fell. Hundreds of thousands of Chinese were killed. The massacre of

Chinese civilians at Nanjing began in December 1937. In three months, Japanese soldiers killed two hundred thousand civilians and raped twenty thousand women. The Japanese commander at Nanjing, General Iwane Matsui, was later hanged as a war criminal. By the end of 1938, Japan controlled most of eastern China. The Chinese Army was forced to withdraw to Sichuan Province in central China. Japan signed anti-Communist pacts with Germany and Italy.

World War II

China's fortunes improved when the war with Japan became part of World War II. The war began when Germany invaded Poland on September 1, 1939. Germany's dictator, Adolf Hitler, soon conquered most of Europe. In June 1940, Italy joined Germany in the war. In September, Japan signed an agreement that further allied the country with Germany and Italy. Germany invaded the Soviet Union in June 1941.

On December 7, 1941, the Japanese launched a surprise bombing attack on Pearl Harbor, a U.S. naval base in Hawaii. Nineteen ships were sunk. Some twenty-four hundred American soldiers and sailors were killed. In response, the United States declared war on Japan. Because of these events, on December 8, China joined the Allies in World War II. The main members of the Allies were the United States, Great Britain, China, and the Soviet Union. Against them stood Germany, Italy, and Japan, known as the Axis powers.

General Chiang Kai-shek (right) directed China's military forces in the war against Japan.

The Chinese now had the Allies' support against Japan, which was rapidly conquering Southeast Asia and islands in the Pacific. China gained respect among the Allied countries. In 1942, Chiang became the supreme commander of the Allied forces in China. He was one of the four Allied leaders, who also included Prime Minister Winston Churchill of Great Britain, Josef Stalin of the Soviet Union, and President Franklin D. Roosevelt of the United States. Support from the United States aided the Chinese. U.S. major general Joseph W. Stilwell served as Chiang's chief of staff and helped to train the Chinese Army. The United States trained Chinese men as pilots and established an air force in China.

World War II ended after U.S. president Harry Truman, who replaced Roosevelt in 1945, ordered the dropping of atomic bombs on two Japanese cities. Bombs were dropped on Hiroshima and Nagasaki on August 6 and August 9, 1945, respectively. Over two hundred forty thousand Japanese civilians were killed in the bombings. Japan was defeated. Yet the war inflicted huge casualties on China. Some 20 million Chinese died in the fighting. Millions of Chinese starved because the Japanese took their food supplies. China's economy was in tatters. Riots and strikes disrupted the cities.

Civil War, 1946–1949

With the Japanese defeat, China was no longer united against a common foreign foe. Tensions rose between the Communists and Guomindang. To avert more war, Truman sent U.S. general George C. Marshall to China to help the two sides reach a settlement. The Marshall peace talks were unsuccessful. In March 1946, an all-out civil war erupted. The Soviet Union backed the Communists, while the United States supported the Guomindang.

During World War II, the Communist party had grown stronger, particularly in the countryside. Many Chinese had suffered so extremely that they had lost faith in the Guomindang. The Communists now controlled a large area in northern China, once occupied by the Japanese. But the Red Army still had fewer men and arms than the Guomindang. Even the Soviet leader Stalin urged Mao to dissolve his army and join Chiang's government, but Mao refused.

Chiang Flees to Taiwan

Slowly, the Red Army built up strength. More peasants rallied behind the Communists. When the Red Army seized an area, they took land belonging to landlords and gave it to poor farmers. When Guomindang commanders surrendered, they were sometimes allowed to become officers in the Red Army. In 1947, the Communists launched offensives and began scoring victories.

By 1949, the Communists had finally defeated the Guomindang. Chiang Kai-shek fled with some 2 million refugees to Taiwan, a mountainous island one hundred miles off the China coast. Taiwan had been a Japanese colony since 1895. After World War II, China was given control over the island. In 1949, Chiang took over, brutally imposing martial law. There, he established the Republic of China. Many Taiwanese were killed during the first years of his rule. Gradually, Taiwan, which became known as Nationalist China, moved forward toward democracy and economic stability. But mainland China refused to recognize Taiwan's independence, maintaining it was a breakaway province.

The Red Army marched triumphantly into Beijing. The Communists were determined to unify China. They also had to help China recover from war. People needed to work and eat. With Mao as leader, this would not be an ordinary recovery effort.

A New China

Early in the morning of October 1, 1949, crowds poured into Tiananmen Square, the open plaza at the edge of the Forbidden City in Beijing. The Forbidden City is a sprawling complex of buildings, gardens, courtyards, and lakes. It was built in the fifteenth century to house and protect the emperors of the Ming dynasty. The emperors were long gone. A spirit of festivity and celebration swept the square. Chinese military planes flew overhead in a blue autumn sky. Flags and banners flapped in the breeze.

At ten o'clock in the morning, Mao Zedong stood atop Tiananmen Gate, the Gate of Heavenly Peace, marking the entrance to the Forbidden City. At six feet tall, Mao was an imposing figure. Yet he wore a modest dark suit and simple worker's cap. Surrounded by senior leaders of the Chinese Communist party, he spoke into a tall microphone.

Mao announced the formation of the People's Republic of China (PRC). China had been dominated for centuries by emperors. Foreign invaders had exploited its resources. Civil war had torn it apart. Now a new era had begun. "The Chinese people have stood up," Mao declared. China would no longer be subject to insult and humiliation, he said. The crowd shouted "Long Live the People's Republic of China" and filled the square with other slogans and revolutionary songs. The five-star flag of the PRC was raised.

Source Document

From now on our nation will belong to the community of the peace-loving and freedom-loving nations of the world and work courageously and industriously to foster its own civilization and well-being and at the same time to promote world peace and freedom. Ours will no longer be a nation subject to insult and humiliation. We have stood up.[1]

Mao gave his speech, "The Chinese People Have Stood Up!," on September 21, 1949, during his address at the First Plenary Session of the Chinese People's Political Consultative Conference.

Bright Hopes

Many years later, Mao's personal physician, Dr. Li Zhisui, remembered that day. He had listened to Mao's words with great hope. "I was so full of joy my heart nearly burst out of my throat, and tears welled up in my eyes. I was so proud of China, so full of hope, so happy that the exploitation and suffering, the aggression from foreigners would be gone forever," he observed.[2]

The Chinese people called the revolution, the "liberation." Mao promised that the old lines between landlords and peasants would disappear. People would work together as equals for the common good. China would be transformed from a land of poor farmers into a modern industrialized nation. Chinese who had left during the civil war soon returned to their country.

Mao was not a young man in 1949. He was fifty-six years old. He had spent much of his youth as a revolutionary and soldier, fighting against those in power. Now he was in charge. He was about to embark on a very different and difficult challenge: leading a troubled nation of over 400 million people.

Soviet Support

Mao needed support from outside China. The Cold War, or the rivalry between groups of Communist and non-Communist nations that had developed after World War II, was under way. To gain power, nations had to align with either the Soviet Union, which led the Eastern bloc of Communist nations, or the United States and its democratic allies, known as the Western bloc. The Soviets had supported the Chinese Communists for decades. Now Mao needed their help once again.

Soon after the Communist victory, Mao traveled to the Soviet Union. He met with Soviet leader Josef Stalin to seek support. In February 1950, China and the Soviet Union signed the Treaty of Friendship, Alliance and Mutual Assistance. The two countries pledged to come to each other's aid if attacked. Yet the treaty was not entirely equal. It gave the Soviets certain economic rights in China, such as allowing Soviet companies to exploit mineral resources in Manchuria. The treaty also gave independence to Outer Mongolia, a region that China long considered as its own. Still, the Soviet Union was China's only major ally.

The Korean War

Soon China was swept into war again. In October 1950, Mao's army invaded its neighbor to the west, Tibet, which had an uneasy relationship with China. A Communist government led by Chinese officials was installed. Tibetans were compelled to raise red flags and Mao posters in their homes. The deeply religious people were forced to give up their Buddhist practices, and their temples were destroyed.

More trouble occurred on China's northeast coast, where the Korean peninsula extends. For more than one thousand years, the small country of Korea was unified and independent. But in the late 1800s, China, Russia, and Japan fought to control Korea. In 1910, Japan declared Korea part of the Japanese Empire. After Japan lost World War II, the Allies agreed to restore Korean independence in a cooperative manner. But relations between the Allied countries quickly deteriorated. Korea was split in half. A democratic government allied with the United States was established in the south. The Soviets backed the Communist government in the north.

Civil war broke out when North Korean troops invaded South Korea on June 25, 1950. The war became an international conflict between Communist and non-Communist countries. Mao needed Korea as a Communist ally. On October 25, 1950, Chinese troops crossed the Yalu River into North Korea. All told, China sent more than 2.3 million troops to support North Korea. On the other side, Japan, the United States, and some twenty other countries sent arms and men to South Korea. After fierce fighting and heavy casualties on both sides, a truce that permanently divided North Korea and South Korea was signed in July 1953. Neither side could claim a victory.

The war effort helped unify China. However, it fed anti-American sentiment among the Chinese people. China was also condemned by the United Nations (UN). China had lost 1 million soldiers, including Mao's son, Mao Anying. Mao Anying was twenty-eight years old and a volunteer in Korea assigned to

Workers in a factory write a letter to Mao, pledging to work harder to support Chinese troops in Korea. The factory was a supplier of uniforms and bedding to the soldiers.

headquarters as a staff officer and Russian interpreter. On November 25, 1950, his offices were hit by a U.S. and UN bomb, and he was killed. Mao ordered that Anying's body remain in North Korea as a symbol of his duty to China. "In war there must be sacrifice. Without sacrifice there will be no victory. There are no parents in the world who do not treasure their children," said Mao.[3]

Economic Development

With the end of the Korean War, China began to rebuild its economy. Decades of war had left it in shambles. When Chiang Kai-shek fled to Taiwan, he took China's gold reserves, and many business owners followed him. Railways and shipping harbors had to be rebuilt. Trade needed to be established.

Railways, shipping companies, and other industries were now owned by the government, not by individuals. The state was the main employer. People were paid according to how much basic necessities, like rice or oil, they could buy with their salaries. To control inflation, or the rising cost of living, the government took over the banking system and regulated the trade of goods. The money and trade flow were brought under control, and inflation was reduced.

Reform

Mao also set about reforming the agricultural system. China relied on its land to feed its people, estimated at between 400 and 600 million in the 1950s. Yet no more than 15 percent of China's land is fertile. Even land suitable for planting is vulnerable to droughts and floods. The land, therefore, has to be carefully managed to yield as much food as possible.

Mao wanted to give the land to the peasants. He also wanted to change the balance of power from landlord to peasant. Starting in 1950, Mao ordered the redistribution of land and the elimination of landlords. A reign of terror began. By December 1952, the land had been seized, but only with terrible bloodshed. Landlords were shot and killed in front of crowds of peasants. The families of landlords lost everything.

The peasants, for the first time, had their own small plots, but not for long.

In 1953, Mao launched China's first Five-Year Plan, using the Soviet model for development, to boost both agricultural and industrial production. "What can we make at present? We can make tables and chairs, teacups and teapots, we can grow grain and grind it into flour, and we can make paper. But we can't make a single motor car, plane, tank, or tractor," stated Mao in 1954.[4] Mao encouraged the development of iron, steel, electric power, and machinery industries. The Soviet Union sent money and advisors to help develop heavy industry. In return, China gave the Soviets its grain. This arrangement continued even when famine struck China in the late 1950s.

Mao decided that farmers would do better if they worked together in agricultural collectives. "The only way for the majority of the peasants to shake off poverty, improve their livelihood and fight natural calamities is to unite and go forward along the high road of socialism," stated Mao.[5] Families pooled their equipment and land in hopes of producing many more crops. By 1957, there were nearly eight hundred thousand collective farms.

The New Government

A new government was put into place in Beijing to carry out the many reforms. Its basic structure has remained in place since the 1950s. China was led by three bodies: the Communist party; the State Council that runs the government and the People's Liberation Army, formerly the Red Army. By 1954, Mao was head of all three. He was chairman of the Chinese Communist party, chief of state of the People's Republic of China (PRC), and chairman of the military.

China is governed under a constitution that has evolved over the years. The first constitution was adopted in 1954. The latest was passed in 1982 and amended in 1993. The current Chinese Constitution states, "The PRC is a socialist state under the people's democratic dictatorship led by the working class and based on the alliance of workers and peasants."[6] The people do not vote for their leaders in open democratic elections, as citizens do in the United States. China is basically a one-party system of government, its leaders selected by the Communist party.

While the Communist party and government are separate, the party approves every decision. Elected officials are members of the party. Most important civilian, police, and military jobs are assigned to party members. In the PRC's first years, veterans of the Long March took top government positions. However, only a small percentage of the population belonged to the party. The Communist party had a membership of roughly 4.5 million, mostly peasants, in 1949. Today, about 5 percent of Chinese, over 64.5 million, are members of the party.

Following Lenin's practice in the Soviet Union, the government and Communist party are shaped like pyramids. A few powerful people rule at the top. The party chairman, now called the general secretary, is the leader of the party. Beneath him is the Secretariat, a small group of senior party leaders. The Secretariat has the final say in party decisions. Beneath the Secretariat is the Politburo, the party's inner power circle. The Politburo appoints workers to government, civilian, and military positions. It also establishes policy guidelines. The three-hundred-member Central Committee is under the Politburo. These leaders are elected by the National Party Congress, a larger body with close to two thousand representatives from all regions of China. The National Party Congress meets to vote on party policies and programs, but in truth has little authority. However, future party leaders often emerge from the congress.

China's state is led by a president and vice president, who also hold high positions in the Communist party. The president nominates the premier, who is the head of the government. The premier heads the State Council, made up of representatives from ministries, commissions, and other institutions, which runs the government on a daily basis. In 1949, Zhou Enlai became China's first premier and foreign minister. He was a veteran of the Long March and a longtime party leader. More interested in improving people's lives than strictly following Mao's Communist ideals, Zhou steered Mao away from some of his more radical ideas.

The PRC's Constitution states: "all power in the People's Republic of China belongs to the people."[7] In practice, the people are represented in China's government by the National People's Congress, made up of three thousand delegates elected by local people's congresses in counties and towns across the country. The National People's Congress meets once a year to amend the constitution, enact laws, elect government officials, approve the national economic plan and budget, and make other decisions. Yet the congress usually follows orders from the Communist party's Politburo.

China's large armed forces, which include an army, navy, and air force, are led by the Military Commission of the Communist party and the Central Military Commission of the government. The People's Liberation Army, not only defends the country, it also enforces the Communist party's policies and programs. Many of China's military leaders have been party leaders. Mao relied on the support of the military to carry out his programs.

Public Health

Reaching out to the smallest, most remote village, the massive government bureaucracy unified China for the first time in years. It also exerted strict control over the Chinese people. The government had many problems to tackle. One priority was public health. In the early 1950s, the average Chinese life expectancy was very low. Many children died before reaching adulthood. Mao wanted to improve the health of his people. The government set out to promote basic hygiene, preventive health care, and family planning.

In the past, many Chinese did not have access to medical care. A system of universal access to medical treatment and free preventive care was put into place. Improving the health of rural workers was a priority for Mao. Under his leadership, nearly the entire rural population was provided with virtually free basic health care services. Doctors were sent to the countryside. Clinics and pharmacies were set up even in remote villages.

Mass campaigns were started to fight contagious diseases. Campaigns to vaccinate people helped to nearly wipe out deadly diseases such as cholera, typhoid, and scarlet fever. The incidence of other infectious and parasitic diseases was reduced. Tuberculosis, a major health hazard in 1949, remained a problem to some extent into the 1980s, as did other diseases such as hepatitis, malaria, and dysentery.

Outside the large cities, most of China had no modern sewage system. In rural areas, human waste had always been collected and scattered in the fields as fertilizer. This led to the spread of parasites and disease. To combat this problem, people were ordered to build facilities to treat human waste. Peasants began treating human waste in composting and storage pits, and with chemicals. They were ordered to dig deep wells to access cleaner water. As a result of these and other campaigns, health standards rapidly improved.

Education

Along with improving health, Mao wanted his people educated. Prior to 1949, most peasants could not read. Few peasants were able to take the time away from the fields to learn the thousands of Chinese characters necessary to read and write. Mao wanted every child to have a basic education.

The education system was brought under the central government. New schools were built. Attendance at primary schools rose from 24 million in 1949 to 64 million in 1957. More students attended middle schools, technical schools, and universities, as well. By 1985, about 96 percent of primary school-age children were enrolled in some 832,300 primary schools. Still, many families could not pay the school fees. Children dropped out early. More boys than girls attended school. Thus, more women remained unable to read or write.

Women's Lives Changed

Overall, however, the status of women did improve under Mao. Chinese culture was traditionally centered around men. In ancient China, girls had no names until they married and took their husband's surname. After marriage, the bride joined her husband's family, where she was considered inferior to her mother-in-law and her husband.

Mao liked to say that women hold up half the sky. He outlawed child marriages and arranged marriages, the sale of brides, wife beating, and prostitution. The

1950 Marriage Law did away with the second-class legal status of women. Women could own property and choose their husbands, rather than submit to arranged marriages. They were given equal rights over property and divorce settlements. Girls could attend school, and women worked alongside men in the fields or factories. "In order to build a great socialist society, it is of the utmost importance to arouse the broad masses of women to join in productive activity. Men and women must receive equal pay for equal work in production," Mao wrote.[8]

Women were encouraged to become managers and party officials. Yet women rarely became leaders. With few exceptions, men held the important positions in the party and the government. Women were still responsible for the children and housework. Most women worked while pregnant. Still, families preferred sons, who would carry on the family name.

Religion

The Communist party regarded religion as a threat to the state's authority and a diversion from more important matters. Many Chinese followed the Buddhist or Taoist religions. Some Chinese converted to Christianity under the influence of European missionaries. Others lived according to the teachings of Confucius and ancestor worship, or combined more than one religion. The Communists expected that religious beliefs would just fade away as people became educated and understood the world from a more scientific viewpoint, but meanwhile religion was restricted in the PRC.

The government forbade public religious festivals. During China's land reform in the 1950s, monasteries and temples lost their lands and buildings. Buddhist monks were forced to do nonreligious work. Chinese Protestants and Roman Catholics had to defend their loyalty to the state and party. Catholics, who revered their leader, the pope, were persecuted. The Chinese Catholic Church broke away from the pope in order to show its loyalty to the government.

Thought Reform

People were denied other personal liberties as well. After all, Mao was determined to change society. The individual was less important than the state. During the 1950s, Mao launched the Four Olds campaign to wipe out old ideas, habits, customs and cultures. Another campaign, known as the Three Anti's, was aimed at eliminating waste and corruption in government. The Five Anti's campaign was directed at business owners and wealthy people, to stop bribery, tax fraud, and other cheating. These campaigns aimed to modify people's behavior to benefit the state.

People were not allowed to criticize the government or to question the Communist party. Chinese art, literature, and music had to serve the revolution. Artists and writers were attacked if their work did not appear patriotic. Newspapers and radio broadcasts were carefully checked for anti-Communist sentiment.

Even the party newspaper, *The People's Daily*, was checked for disloyalty. Mao fired the editor for not backing the new government.

Critics of the government were called counterrevolutionaries. They were severely punished. Hundreds of thousands of these people were killed during the PRC's early years, although the exact number is uncertain. Others had to undergo thought reform. People were sent to prison and labor camps for reeducation. Reeducation was a method of imposing Communist party ideas on the people. As China's leader, Mao was following the strong-arm philosophy of legalism. The will of Mao and the Communist party were not to be challenged.

A Changed World

Under Mao, the lives of the Chinese people changed in many ways. People were assigned where to live and what work to do. They needed permission to marry and, later, to have children. This system seemed to offer a great security net. However, in exchange for the promise of security, the people of China lost many personal freedoms. It did not take long for the optimism that swept through China in 1949 to be replaced with a more complicated reality.

Chapter 7

Trouble and Turmoil

Mao recognized that his revolution would not succeed overnight. In a speech in February 1957, "On the Correct Handling of Contradictions among the People," Mao stated that more time was needed to achieve the socialist system. He acknowledged that many Chinese people were still hungry, and that hundreds of thousands had died during the Communist revolution. But, he said, struggle was necessary. One of the ways he would move the revolution forward was to open the gates to criticism.

The Hundred Flowers Movement

For a brief period in 1957, Mao allowed criticism of his government. He decided that limited debates among the masses were helpful. Perhaps more art, literature, and science would be good for China, he thought.

Fresh ideas might improve and unify China. Long suspicious of intellectuals and artists, Mao now hoped to win their support.

Mao suggested that people voice their honest opinions of the government. He persuaded his colleagues to allow intellectuals and non–party members to criticize the party. To launch the campaign, he used this quote from classical Chinese poetry, "Let a hundred flowers bloom, and let a hundred schools of thought contend."[1] He meant that many ideas and opinions could flourish together.

At first, people were fearful of speaking out. In the past, critics had been severely punished. They remembered the campaign against enemies of the state in the early 1950s. Yet by the summer of 1957, people began openly expressing their views. People complained about the government, Marxism, and restrictions on their creative work. Criticisms were posted on public walls and published in national newspapers.

Mao and other officials were surprised by the flood of complaints and accusations. After only a few weeks, Mao brutally retaliated. The critics were labeled "rightists" and enemies of the people and forced to take back what they had said or written. By the fall of 1957, the Anti-Rightist Campaign had silenced Mao's critics. Hundreds of thousands of people lost their jobs, were imprisoned, or were sent to the countryside to do hard labor. Their absence left a huge void. "The cost to China's scientific and economic establishment was as high as it was to the creative arts, literature, and education generally," wrote historian Jonathan Spence.[2] The window of free speech closed as suddenly as it had opened in China.

Great Leap Forward

Hoping to move the economy forward, Mao launched the Second Five-Year Plan in 1957 to improve production in both agriculture and industry. The government also began reforming education to stress science and engineering. Mao wanted China to catch up with industrialized nations, like Great Britain. He wanted major changes in Chinese society, as well.

In February 1958, the National People's Congress announced the start of the "Great Leap Forward." The PRC reorganized rural farmland into People's Communes. Private property was abolished. The state now owned the land and everyone worked together. In the communes, people shared their tools, labor, animals, and land, and farmed the land together, pooling profits. The communes replaced the family unit and the village support system. People gave up their homes and property. Soon, most of China's farmland was divided into communes, each made up of between two thousand and twenty thousand households.

Each commune had its own government and economy. The communes were divided into production brigades and production teams. Men and women worked in the fields, while children were cared for in communal nurseries and attended communal schools. Everyone ate together in communal kitchens. "One

Throughout the years of Mao's leadership farming remained very important to China's survival. In 1967, farmers read from The Thoughts of Mao *before taking part in a harvest.*

village, one stove. Everyone had to eat in the canteen," recalled Wang Jiufu a village party chief in Yan'an.[3] The adults lived in dormitories. Often, the women lived separately from the men.

To further boost the economy, people were ordered to build massive public works projects. Over 100 million people were put to work. They constructed irrigation systems to bring water to farmland. They dug reservoirs to provide water for villages. They built dams. As a result of these huge projects, fields were deserted and the usual labor went neglected.

The Great Leap also called for increases in steel, electricity, and coal production. Mao ordered people in the countryside to build steel furnaces. They were told to melt pots and pans and even rocks that might contain iron ore. Millions of small furnaces were built in the backyards of homes and businesses. The nation's coal went to the furnaces, leaving trains without fuel. But the metal created in backyard furnaces was full of impurities and was therefore useless. "We cooked the rocks day and night for a year and couldn't make one . . . piece of steel!" said Wang Jiufu.[4]

Peasants were urged to assault the "four pests"—rats, sparrows, flies, and mosquitoes—and snails that transmit a serious disease. Children were told to catch flies, which they brought to party officials to be counted. However, the cure was often worse than the problem. By killing the sparrows that eat insects, people were unintentionally allowing flies and mosquitos to multiply.

Disaster Strikes

Despite the labor of millions, the Great Leap Forward was a disaster. Agricultural production increased at first, but fertile land had been lost. The remaining farmland was overused. Crops began to fail. Local commune officials competed against each other. They overestimated their farm production figures. The Communist party then taxed the communes based on the inaccurate figures. Taxes were collected in grain, not money, reducing the amount of grain available for food. People were going hungry.

Mao refused to see what was happening. After traveling around the country, Mao praised the progress he thought he saw. In an interview with a reporter on September 29, 1958, Mao said, "During this trip, I have witnessed the tremendous energy of the masses. On this foundation it is possible to accomplish any task whatsoever."[5] He urged the people to work even harder, and to become even more dedicated to the revolution. To Mao, the transformation of the countryside was a success.

Party leaders were frightened to tell Mao that people were starving. Meanwhile, severe weather worsened China's troubles. In 1959, droughts in some parts of China, and flash floods in other regions, brought crop failures. A terrible famine swept through China. By 1962, up to 30 million people were dead of starvation.

Khrushchev

Mao was also facing the breakdown in China's relationship with its important ally, the Soviet Union. After Stalin's death in 1953, Nikita Khrushchev became the leader of the Soviet Union. Stalin had not always supported the Chinese Communists, particularly before 1949. Still, Mao was angered when Khrushchev turned on Stalin and his programs. In a speech in February 1956, Khrushchev called Stalin a

Mao Zedong and Nikita Khrushchev meet in China in 1958. A few years later, the leaders and their countries would not be as friendly to one another.

murderer and accused him of tyranny and terror. Mao feared that one day people might reject him, as well.

The two countries had other conflicts. The Chinese feared that the Soviets' nuclear weapons program could threaten China's interests. Also, Khrushchev was critical of Mao's economic and social policies. In a serious blow to China, the Soviet Union withdrew its financial aid and advisers in 1960. Without Soviet support, China's recovery from the famine of the late 1950s would be difficult.

Mao Is Overshadowed

In the summer of 1959, party leaders met at Lushan to talk about the Great Leap Forward. The minister of defense, Peng Dehuai, criticized Mao for the economic disaster. Peng was also upset that Mao was breaking ties with the Soviet Union. He believed China needed Soviet support. Angry at the criticism, Mao expelled Peng and his followers from the government. He appointed Lin Biao, a Mao loyalist, as the new defense minister.

Peng was not the only person who thought Mao had made mistakes. Two party leaders, Deng Xiaoping and Liu Shoaqi, were preparing to replace Mao and his radical ideas. Deng was a founder of the Red Army and secretary general of the Communist party since 1954. Liu was the vice president of the People's Republic and second to Mao in leadership. They wanted to concentrate less on political ideas; they instead wanted to build the economy and feed the people.

"They treated me like a dead ancestor," he said of Deng and Liu.[6] Mao had little choice but to give up his power, at least in part. In the spring of 1959, he stepped down as president of the PRC. He remained chairman of the Chinese Communist party. Liu replaced him as leader of the government.

In the next years, Deng worked with Liu and Zhou Enlai, China's premier, to help China recover and restore the people's confidence. Peasants had supported the revolution because it promised them a better life. Under communism, however, no matter how hard they worked, they earned neither more nor less than anyone else. Families wanted their own homes and plots of land. In response, Deng and his colleagues abolished the communes and the backyard furnaces. They returned property to the people. They began to pay workers to produce consumer goods. To revive the economy, the leaders initiated emergency measures such as importing grain from the West. These practical steps were successful. By the mid-1960s, food supplies were back to normal.

Although the economic crisis was over, China would see more dark years under Mao. During the next decade, Mao would take desperate measures to restore his authority. Many Chinese people would suffer terrible losses in Mao's new bid for power.

The Cultural Revolution

Mao had grown frustrated with the slow pace of revolutionary change in China. Many of his ideas about communism and building a new China had not been carried out. In his view, old ideas and customs were still standing in the way of progress. His revolution had stalled.

By the mid-1960s, Mao feared he had lost the respect of his country and his comrades. Important decisions about China's future were being made without him. Mao questioned his colleagues' devotion to the revolution. He saw that the moderate party leaders were taking China in a new direction, away from his vision. He was also uneasy with intellectuals, whose ideas threatened his authority.

In Mao's view, revolution was an ongoing struggle, without an end. Now he began to stir up conflict again.

88

He called the new upheaval the Great Proletarian Cultural Revolution. With the support of the People's Liberation Army, Mao set out to destroy his enemies and all that was traditional in China.

The New Revolution

Mao was determined to destroy the Four Olds—the old ideas, old customs, old culture, and old habits. According to Mao, the bourgeoisie, or middle class, was using the Four Olds to corrupt the masses and capture their minds. He called on the masses to lead his newest battle. "Trust the masses, rely on them, and respect their initiative, cast out fear and don't be afraid of disturbances," he said.[1]

On August 18, 1966, Mao stood again at Beijing's Tiananmen Square. Before him were hundreds of thousands of young people chanting revolutionary slogans. The crowd was made up of Red Guards, Mao's new troops. Dressed in military uniforms with red armbands, the Red Guards were mostly teenagers. Mao wore the green uniform of the People's Liberation Army and the PLA cap with the red star. He did not speak, but rather let the army leader, Lin Biao, address the crowd for him.

Many people in the crowd waved a small red book, *Quotations from Chairman Mao Tse-tung*. Better known as *The Little Red Book*, it was compiled by Lin in the early 1960s and published in 1966. The pages contained hundreds of excerpts from Mao's writings and speeches. The book's slogans would be memorized

A group of children reads from The Little Red Book *during the Cultural Revolution.*

by millions of Chinese. As Mao looked out on the sea of faces, a young girl presented him with a Red Guard armband. This gesture symbolized that the founder of the People's Republic was now commanding a new army.

Red Guards

Mao turned to young people to lead his new revolution. Schools were closed. Students put away their books to form Red Guard units. Teenagers flooded into Beijing to join the Red Guards, and more huge rallies were held in Tiananmen Square. Mao opened the railroads to free passage. Red Guards from Beijing traveled in squads to spread the Cultural Revolution to the rest of China.

The Red Guards followed the "four big rights"— the right to speak out freely, air views fully, hold great debates, and write "big character posters." They wrote criticisms of people on the huge posters, which were hung on public walls for everyone to see. Everything changed, even the names of streets and businesses. In Changsha, for example, a park was renamed "People's Park" and a shop hung out a new sign: "The East Is Red Food Store." "All this was extremely confusing, especially for the old people, and everybody was always getting off at the wrong bus stop and getting lost," Liang Heng describes in his memoir, *Son of the Revolution*.[2] Even babies were given revolutionary names.

The traditional respect for the hierarchy of society, a part of the Confucian value system, disappeared. Children were told to turn on their parents for their old thoughts and customs. They forced their grandparents out to sweep the streets. Students criticized their teachers. Even doctors, held in deep regard in China, were denounced and humiliated.

Millions were caught up in the frenzy. As in other countries in the 1960s, the young people were rebelling against traditions. In addition, many of them loved and idolized Mao. They were willing to do anything for his approval. Jung Chang, in her memoir *Wild Swans*, describes her excitement at joining the Red Guards. She was proud of her Red Guard armband with its gold characters. "I was not forced to join the Red Guards. I was keen to do so. . . . it never occurred to me to question the Cultural Revolution or the Red Guards. . . . They were Mao's creations, and Mao was beyond contemplation," she recalled.[3]

Destruction

Encouraged by Mao, the Red Guards launched a campaign of destruction. "Mao had found his new guerrilla army to assault the political heights. A whole generation of young Chinese was ready to die, and to kill, for him, with unquestioning obedience. And kill they did," wrote Mao biographer Philip Short.[4] The police supplied the Red Guards with names of people who were enemies of the party. The Red Guards tore apart their homes, searching for objects that they felt represented old culture.

People accused of being rightists, landlords, rich peasants, or traitors faced humiliation or much worse. Sometimes they had to walk through the streets wearing tall dunce caps. Some were killed. Others were sent to the countryside to do hard labor. "The number of victims from the uncoordinated violence of the Cultural Revolution is incalculable, but there were many millions," wrote historian Jonathan Spence.[5]

Professionals such as teachers and writers were considered threats to the revolution. Lao She, author of a best-selling book, *Rickshaw Boy,* was seized by the Red Guards. He was taken to the courtyard of a public building in Beijing. There, he and other writers and artists were given yin-yang haircuts—meaning only half their heads were shaved. Black ink was poured over their faces. The Red Guards beat them violently, then sent them home. Like many victims during that time, Lao She, at sixty-seven, could not endure the shame. The following day, he drowned himself in a local lake.

Struggle Meetings

The targets of the Red Guards often had to attend "struggle meetings" in large community buildings or arenas. They were forced to stand on public platforms and read a "self-criticism," or confession. The crowd heckled and jeered the victim, even a friend, relative, or neighbor. The victims often collapsed on stage or were beaten by the crowd. The purpose was to exhaust and humiliate the victims, both physically and mentally.

Some victims lived to tell their story. Nien Cheng was the widow of an official of Chiang Kai-shek's government and an employee of Shell Oil. In August 1966, Red Guards arrested her for being a spy. She was imprisoned in solitary confinement for more than six years. During that time, she underwent interrogation and struggle meetings. In her memoir, *Life and Death in Shanghai*, Cheng describes a struggle meeting: "[T]he audience jumped up from their seats when the speaker told them I was a spy for the imperialists. They expressed their anger and indignation by crowding around me to shout abuse," she recalls.[6] She was forced to stand in the jet position, with her hands raised painfully, while her head was bowed. Having done nothing wrong, Cheng refused to confess she was an enemy of the state.

Books and Religion

Mao considered China's cultural treasures to be obstacles to progress. Although he was a poet and his study was filled with books, he encouraged the destruction of literature. The Red Guards burned books in public bonfires. Music and art were also destroyed. The Red Guards smashed musical instruments. They raided the opera house and museums in Beijing, destroying costumes, stage props, swords, and priceless objects.

The Communists had always been wary of organized religion and its sway on the population. Now

In this propaganda poster, members of the Red Guard yield tools of agriculture and industry as they step on and burn items symbolizing old religion and literature. The guard members also carry Communist books and flags, including one that features a portrait of Mao.

they took sledgehammers to the shrines of Confucius. Red Guards burned Buddhist temples and hacked down statues honoring family ancestors.

Red Guards arrived in Tibet in July 1966. In 1959, a failed uprising against Chinese rule had left tens of thousands of Tibetans dead and led to the exile of the Tibetan spiritual leader, the Dalai Lama, to India. The Red Guards enlisted young Tibetans in the

Cultural Revolution. From 1966 to 1969, the young rebels destroyed monasteries, temples, and other holy sites. It was not until the 1980s that monasteries were allowed to open and religious life resumed in Tibet. Tibet was still under Chinese rule in 2003, and an international Free Tibet movement continued.

Also during the 1960s, the government sent young revolutionaries to rural areas to dispense medical care. The "barefoot doctors" lived in villages and provided basic medical care. They carried their medical kits over their shoulders. When they were not working in medicine, they toiled with the peasants in the rice paddies. By the early 1970s, there were almost 2 million barefoot doctors. While they improved health care, they also helped increase the wide reach of the Communist state.

The Cult of Mao

In the cities of China, loudspeakers awoke people at dawn with the song, "The East Is Red." The tune was from an old Chinese folk song. The lyrics were rewritten to glorify Mao and the Communist revolution. Like most of the music promoted by the PRC, the song was propaganda. It was sung to arouse enthusiasm for the revolution and devotion to Mao.

Mao's picture hung on buildings, in public squares, and in private homes. People greeted each other with praises to Mao and carried copies of *The Little Red Book*. When couples got married, they did so in front of his portrait. In schools that remained open, students

Source Document

The East is Red

1

The East is red, the sun has risen,
China has made a Mao Zedong.
He creates fortune for the people,
Hu er hai yue*, he's the saviour of them all!

2

Chairman Mao loves the people,
He is our guiding leader,
Leading us forward,
Hu er hai yue, to develop New China!

3

The Communist Party is like the sun,
It brightens up everything it shines.
Where there is the Communist Party,
Hu er hai yue, people will be liberated.[7]

*An English translation could not be found for this phrase.

Based on a traditional Chinese folk tune, the national anthem of the Cultural Revolution was given new lyrics extolling Mao Zedong and the Communist regime.

started the day by bowing to his portrait. They studied Mao's thought and recited pledges of loyalty like this one: "A long, long life to Chairman Mao. Chairman Mao, you are the red sun in our hearts. We are sun flowers. Sun flowers always face the red sun. We think of you day and night. We wish you a long life."[8]

By the late 1960s, Mao had become like a Chinese emperor. While his revolution was for the masses, Mao lived in relative luxury in his elegant quarters in the Forbidden City in Beijing. He swam in his private

This poster shows the Chinese people admiring Mao and his beliefs. However, many historians feel that Mao gained much of his support by playing on the fears of the people.

swimming pool. He traveled in a private train, rarely mingling with the Chinese people. People quickly agreed with him, mostly out of fear. "Mao was a dictator. There were no other preferences but his. Those of us around him had to grant his every wish. To assert one's individuality in Mao's imperial court would have been an invitation to disaster," wrote Dr. Li Zhisui, Mao's doctor.[9]

Yet Mao still seemed insecure. Fearful of betrayals, he fired his secretaries and aides. Some were sent to prison. Mao accused old comrades of pushing China toward capitalism and undermining the revolution. No one, it seemed, was safe from Mao's attacks.

Fallen Leaders

Pu Yi, the emperor who had been expelled in 1924, was persecuted during the Cultural Revolution. He later worked as a gardener and died in 1967, marking the end of a dynasty that had fallen long before.

Mao set out to restore his authority by going after moderate party leaders. He accused them of taking the so-called capitalist road. Deng Xiaoping, general secretary of the Communist party, was denounced for promoting capitalism. In October 1969, Deng, who had survived the Long March, was exiled to Nanchang, in Jiangxi Province, where he was heavily guarded. He worked as a laborer in a tractor plant.

Another important official, Liu Shaoqi, named head of state in 1959 and Mao's chosen successor, suffered even more. He was expelled from the

Communist party and stripped of his government posts. Like the lives of many party leaders, his life was destroyed. Abandoned by his old friends, he saw his children join the Red Guards. Liu was forced to admit to many "crimes" against communism. Without medical treatment, he died in 1969 of pneumonia in a provincial prison.

Madame Mao

Mao's fourth wife, Jiang Qing, became increasingly influential. In 1937, she had joined the Communists in Yan'an, after which she met and married Mao. Jiang's views were even more extreme than Mao's. Known as Madame Mao, she was willing to do anything to stay in power. She turned her attention to China's cultural heritage as a tool for the revolution.

Elaborate and colorful operas have a popular tradition in China. Jiang decided to revolutionize the Beijing Opera by replacing the traditional operas with works emphasizing Mao's doctrine. She banned all cultural expressions except six revolutionary operas. The works expressed the themes of the Cultural Revolution, such as struggle, criticism, and rehabilitation.

People flocked to see the operas. In her memoir, *Red Azalea*, writer Anchee Min describes her love of the operas as a girl:

> I became an opera fan. There were not many forms of entertainment. The word "entertainment" was considered a dirty bourgeois word. The opera was something else. It was a proletarian statement.

The revolutionary operas created by Madam Mao, Comrade Jiang Ching. To love or not love the operas was a serious political attitude. It meant to be or not to be a revolutionary.[10]

The operas did stir up patriotism. Jiang and her closest allies, Zhang Chunqiao, Yao Wenyuan, and Wang Hongwen, gained power. They became known as the Gang of Four. Along with Lin Biao, the defense minister, they held great influence on Mao.

Jiang was ruthless. She attacked anyone who she felt posed a threat to her or Mao's power. A *Time* magazine reporter described her as "the fire-breathing dragon lady of the Cultural Revolution."[11]

Order Returns Slowly

China had fallen into civil disorder. People could not buy basic goods like sugar, salt, and soap. Even those who had, at first, supported Mao's new revolution were dismayed. "All the things I loved were disappearing. The saddest thing of all for me was the ransacking of the library: the golden tiled roof, the delicately sculpted windows, the blue painted chairs. . . . Bookshelves were turned upside down . . ."[12] wrote Jung Chang, a former member of the Red Guard. Her father, a loyal Communist official, was beaten and put in detention after he refused to work with a local official. "Human anguish did not concern Mao," wrote Chang.[13]

Even Mao could no longer ignore the upheaval. Factions of the Red Guards were fighting each other.

The military was getting involved. The violence was threatening to throw the country into anarchy, or civil chaos. To regain control, in July 1968, Mao disbanded the Red Guards. Some 10 million Red Guards were sent to work as peasants, cleaning latrines and working the fields in rural villages.

The Cultural Revolution officially ended in April 1969 with the meeting of the Ninth Communist Party Congress. Mao reclaimed the party leadership. A new party Constitution was passed, which stressed Mao's thought and class struggle. In 1970, Mao was named supreme commander of the nation and the army. He was securely the leader of China once more.

After the Red Guards disbanded, China remained in the grips of chaos. The Gang of Four exerted control until 1976. Production had fallen in most industries. Millions had lost their homes, possessions, and jobs. The young people of this era became known as the "lost generation." They had spent their youths inciting violence or fleeing from it. They lacked the education or job training to build their futures because many had left school to join the Red Guard. The state of the "lost generation" would lead to problems in the years to come.

Chapter 9

Opening the Doors

One of Mao's final achievements was to open the doors of diplomacy to the United States and the West. During most of his life, Mao had rejected the outside world. He had returned China to the isolation of its imperial past. He took only two trips outside China, both to the Soviet Union.

Yet times had changed. By the 1970's, Mao needed a strong ally to help shield against the Soviet Union's aggression and growing nuclear capabilities. Richard M. Nixon, the U.S. president from 1969 to 1974, wanted to build relations with China. He considered China an important player in the balance of world power. "Mainland China, outside the world community, completely isolated, with its leaders not in communication with world leaders, would be a danger to the whole world. . . . So consequently, this step must be taken now," said Nixon in July 1971.[1]

Growing Soviet Threat

Building bridges would take delicate political maneuvering. The United States and China had been enemies since the Korean War. Their relationship worsened during the Vietnam conflict. The small southeast Asian nation, divided between north and south, was embroiled in the Vietnam War from 1957 to 1975. China supported Communist North Vietnam against South Vietnam and the United States. As many as fifty thousand Chinese soldiers were killed in North Vietnam.

Both China and the United States wanted to find a way to end the conflict in Vietnam. President Nixon thought that friendship with China would help reduce Soviet influence and force the Soviets to agree to limit nuclear weapons. The two countries made overtures to each other in the late 1960s and early 1970s. For example, Nixon stated publicly that he wanted to visit China. "If there is anything I want to do before I die, it is to go to China," Nixon told *Time* magazine in 1970.[2] The question was how to make the visit a reality. The two leaders got help from an unexpected corner, the sport of table tennis.

Table-Tennis Diplomacy

Table tennis, known by a leading brand that make's the sport's equipment, Ping-Pong™, was probably introduced to China by British Army officers at the turn of the twentieth century. During the 1950s, Mao's government encouraged it as a national sport in which Chinese athletes could excel at the international level. China's effort to build national pride through table tennis was a huge success. Chinese players have won more gold and silver medals at the Summer Olympics than players from any other nation. Table tennis is also a popular sport among the Chinese people.

In the early 1970s, table tennis formed a diplomatic bridge. Chinese and American teams attended the 31st World Table Tennis Championship in Japan in April 1971. The Americans were invited to play in China following the tournament. The players were the first Americans allowed into China for a cultural exchange since the Communist takeover in 1949. During their historic visit, the players performed exhibition matches. They also saw a little of China, which had been off-limits to the West. The athletes visited the Great Wall of China, met with Chinese students and factory workers, and attended the Canton Ballet.

Premier Zhou Enlai hosted a banquet for the Americans in the Great Hall of the People in Beijing. "You have opened a new chapter in the relations of the American and Chinese people," he declared. "I am confident that this beginning again of our friendship will certainly meet with majority support of our two peoples."[3] The United States announced it planned to remove a two-decades-long embargo, or ban, on trade with China. Not long afterward, the Chinese table-tennis team visited the United States.

Nixon's Visit

The United States and China saw an opportunity for a new relationship. In July 1971, Zhou Enlai met secretly in Beijing with Henry A. Kissinger, assistant to the president for national security affairs. Their talks laid the groundwork for a meeting between Nixon and Mao. Then in August 1971, Taiwan's seat in the United Nations was given to mainland China. This was a historic move since it meant that the United Nations no longer recognized Taiwan as an independent nation. The fact that the United States did not object to this was an encouraging sign to the People's Republic.

On February 21, 1972 , President Nixon and his wife, Patricia, arrived on the presidential airplane, Air Force One, at Beijing Airport. Nixon stepped down from the plane and shook hands with Zhou. Nixon was accompanied by Kissinger, U.S. secretary of state William Rogers, and other American officials. That same day, Nixon and Kissinger met with Mao and Zhou in Mao's private study in Zhongnanhai, his quarters in the Forbidden City.

The conversation between the two world leaders was informal. They sat in armchairs in a half circle in the room where books spilled from the bookcases. Mao did not appear healthy; his speech had been affected by a heart attack in the spring of 1971. He needed two people to help him get up from his armchair. He shuffled when he walked. Still, Mao made a few jokes to put Nixon at ease. He made a strong

The meeting between Richard Nixon and Mao was a big step forward for the relationship between the United States and China.

impression. Kissinger later wrote that the Chinese leader lived "in a style as remote and exalted as any of the emperors."[4]

The meeting signaled that the longtime foes were willing to find common ground. In Shanghai, Zhou and Nixon signed the Joint Communique of the People's Republic of China and the United States of America, an important step toward normalizing relations and reducing tensions in Asia. The communique stated that the leaders agreed to broaden understanding between the two countries. Nixon's visit paved the

Source Document

There are essential differences between China and the United States in their social systems and foreign policies. However, the two sides agreed that countries, regardless of their social systems, should conduct their relations on the principles of respect for the sovereignty and territorial integrity of all states, non-aggression against other states, non-interference in the internal affairs of other states, equality and mutual benefit, and peaceful coexistence. International disputes should be settled on this basis, without resorting to the use or threat of force. The United States and the People's Republic of China are prepared to apply these principles to their mutual relations.[5]

The Joint Communique of the People's Republic of China and the United States of America established friendlier relations between the two nations.

way for future U.S. presidents to work with China. In 1979, the United States established diplomatic relations with China.

Nixon's China trip gave the world a glimpse of a country long hidden behind the "bamboo wall" of communism. (Bamboo is a type of woody grass that is common in China.) Millions of people read journalists' accounts of the Nixons attending a Beijing Opera with Mao's wife, Jiang. The Nixons also walked along the Great Wall of China. "A people that can build a wall like this certainly have a great past to be proud of, and a people who have this kind of a past must also have a great future," commented Nixon to a reporter.[6] In a gesture of friendship, the Chinese sent the United States a pair of giant pandas, Ling-Ling and Hsing-Hsing. The pandas, a rare species endangered by poaching and loss of bamboo forest habitat, were delivered to the National Zoo in Washington, D.C. Millions of Americans came to see them. The pandas were a symbol of the growing goodwill between China and the United States.

Lin Biao

China's international status had improved, but its leadership was in turmoil. Mao had failed to regain his authority, and power struggles raged over his successor. Prior to Nixon's visit, in mid-1971, Mao lost a close supporter. Lin Biao, the loyal army commander, was officially in line to be Mao's successor. After some of his generals were accused of violating party unity, Lin realized that Mao had lost confidence in him. His political future was ruined. While historians are not certain exactly what happened, Lin and other army members may have devised a plan to assassinate Mao by blowing up his train. Then Lin presumably planned to take over the government.

Lin Biao (center) published The Little Red Book *for Mao in 1966. Here, a crowd waves copies of the book as Mao and Lin pass by on October 9, 1970. Less than a year later, Lin would be connected to a plot to assassinate Mao.*

The plot was apparently discovered. Lin and his family fled from China in an air force plane. The plane crashed in Mongolia in September 1971, and everyone onboard was killed. In retribution for Lin's betrayal and flight from China, Mao reduced the power of the army. China now had no one in line to succeed Mao.

Mao's health was declining. Medical tests in 1974 indicated that Mao had a disease called amyotrophic lateral sclerosis (ALS), also known as Lou Gehrig's disease. ALS causes degeneration of the nerve cells in parts of the brain and spinal cord that control a person's voluntary muscles. There is no known cause or cure for ALS. While the disease leaves a person's mind and senses intact, it weakens and paralyzes the muscles. Most people with ALS die of lung failure within a few years. Mao gradually lost his ability to speak, walk, write, and engage in other daily activities.

The Death of Zhou Enlai

The men who had built the PRC were aging. Zhou Enlai, premier of China since 1949, died of cancer in January 1976. Deeply admired by the Chinese people, Zhou was a voice of restraint during Mao's reign. The people of China loved and respected Zhou, but the government forbade the public mourning of his death.

The Qing Ming Festival, on April 5, is a traditional day in China for remembering the dead. On April 4, 1976, crowds of people gathered at the Revolutionary Martyr's Memorial in Tiananmen Square to lay wreaths and poems for Zhou. After the government closed the square, angry throngs broke through the barriers. The government stepped in, arresting and possibly killing some demonstrators. Two days later, former Red Guards and workers demonstrated in Tiananmen Square. They demanded an end to the Cultural Revolution and the Gang of Four. It was the first show of public rebellion since the Communists took over China.

Mao's Death

Mao was last seen in public on May 1, 1976, a day to honor the revolution. For a few moments, he sat overlooking Tiananmen Square and watched a display of fireworks. He suffered three heart attacks in the next few months. After drifting into a coma, he died on September 9, 1976, surrounded by members of the politburo and Dr. Li. Mao was eighty-two years old.

The news of Mao's death traveled quickly. "Funeral music followed today's announcement broadcast over the Peking radio, and 2,000 people gathered in the vast Tienanmen Square, many wearing black armbands, some weeping. Flags fluttered at half staff," wrote a *Reuters* reporter who was in Beijing that day. The announcement made over a loudspeaker proclaimed, "All victories of the Chinese people were achieved under the leadership of Chairman Mao."[7] Funeral music was played on the radio for days.

Writer Anchee Min recalled her feelings at the time. "The reddest sun dropped from the sky of the Middle Kingdom," she wrote. Like millions of others, she wore white paper flowers in her braids in mourning. "Overnight the country became an ocean of white paper flowers. Mourners beat their heads against the door, on grocery-store counters and on walls. Devastating grief," she wrote.[8]

Now, China had to find its way after the death of Mao Zedong.

Chapter 10

The Legacy of Mao's Revolution

The death of Mao left China without a clear map to chart its future. The turmoil of the Cultural Revolution had not yet settled. His Communist revolution was incomplete. It would be up to other leaders, willing to abandon Mao's rigid ways, to forge a new path for China. Soon after Mao died, the party and government ushered in a new era of change and openness.

Economic Revival

The Cultural Revolution's aftermath ended when Mao's wife, Jiang, and her close allies were arrested in October 1976. Jiang had hoped to succeed Mao, but her unpopularity made that impossible. It took four years for the Gang of Four to be brought to trial for a series of crimes, including treason. At the public trial in 1980, Jiang was defiant and proud. She shouted to the judge, "Long live the Revolution!"[1] Sentenced to death, her term was changed to life in prison in 1983. According to reports, she committed suicide in prison in 1991.

The Chinese Communist party made its official judgment on Mao in June 1981 at the Eleventh Party Congress. They praised him for unifying China and establishing the PRC. Later, on July 1 at the celebration of the sixtieth anniversary of the party, Chairman Hu Yaobang stated: "He made immense contributions to the liberation of all oppressed peoples of the world and to human progress."[2] However, for the first time, Mao was officially criticized for his mistakes. The Cultural Revolution was condemned.

Meanwhile, Deng Xiaoping and others banished in the Cultural Revolution were reinstated in the party. By 1980, Deng, the popular moderate, was the leader of China. He rejected many of Mao's ideas in favor of modernizing the economy and opening China to the world. Deng seemed to combine communism and capitalism. The latter is an economic system in which investment and ownership of production and wealth is held by individuals or corporations, not the state. Less interested in ideology than Mao, Deng wanted to improve the lives of his people. "This is the only road China can take. Other roads would only lead to poverty and backwardness," he told *Time* magazine in 1986.[3] The communes were abolished. People were allowed to open restaurants, beauty parlors, and

Source Document

Comrade Mao, like many great historical figures of the past, was not free from shortcomings and mistakes. The principal shortcoming occurred during his later years when, due to long and ardent support by the party and by all the people, he became smug and increasingly and seriously lost contact with realities and the masses. . . . Nevertheless, though Comrade Mao committed serious errors in his late years, it is clear that from the perspective of his entire life his contributions to the Chinese revolution far outweigh his mistakes.[4]

This excerpt is from a speech made by Hu Yaobang, chairman of the Chinese Communist party, on July 1, 1981. Though the speech partially criticized Mao, it was intended to celebrate the sixtieth anniversary of the founding of the Chinese Communist party.

hotels. Foreign investors could import raw materials and goods into special economic zones. Students went abroad to study science and technology. China became one of the fastest-growing economies in the world.

Legacy of a Leader

China has moved beyond Mao's vision. Yet the legacy of his achievements, and his mistakes, still lingers. By isolating China for over two decades, Mao allowed it to lag behind progress made in other countries. At home, Mao's radical ideas often turned into disasters. Millions of people suffered and died in his experiments, like the Great Leap Forward. During the Cultural Revolution, he turned the enthusiasm of China's youth into a storm of destruction. His brutal persecution of intellectuals, writers, artists, and anyone who dared disagree with him, robbed China of much of its cultural wealth and talent.

Yet Mao's energy and ideas, especially as a young man, led China to break away from its past. He rescued China from years of corrupt imperial rule, foreign domination, and civil war. The Communist revolution succeeded, in large part, due to Mao's tactics of guerrilla warfare and peasant support. Mao unified China under a central government in Beijing, which sought to provide people with basic necessities. Improvements in health and education were begun by Mao. Under his leadership, the country moved from a backward nation of peasants to a nuclear power with a growing industrial base and economy. Mao helped China emerge from isolation by reaching out to the United States.

Recently, Mao's radical ideas have been replaced by the passions of nationalism, or pride in China's growth as a nation. Mao's successors, beginning with Deng Xiaoping, led China in rapid economic growth. In 2001, China was admitted to the World Trade Organization, a step toward fuller participation in the global economy. Capitalism is increasingly accepted as the way to China's future.

As the twenty-first century unfolds, many of the social and political restrictions of Mao's Communist state remain in place. Chinese people lack many individual rights taken for granted by Americans, such as freedom of speech. The question is whether greater economic freedom can exist without greater political freedom. "Traveling one road in economics and a different one in politics makes for neither a smooth ride nor a settled destination," wrote China expert Ross Terrill in 2002.[5]

Whatever choices China makes, its future promises to be as dynamic and unique as its past. The eightieth anniversary of the founding of the Chinese Communist party in 2001 coincided with Beijing's bid to host the 2008 summer Olympic games. The news that the Olympics would be held in China was met with much joy across the nation. It was one more sign that China is embracing change and growth. The world's understanding of Mao and the Chinese revolution will continue to grow as well.

Timeline

1883—Mao Zedong is born on December 26.

1894 –1895—War with Japan forces the Chinese to recognize Japan's control over Korea; China gives Japan the island of Taiwan.

1899 –1900—During the Boxer Rebellion, peasant protests against Christian missionaries in China turn violent.

1908—Deaths of the Qing Empress Dowager Cixi and Emperor Guangxu; The last Chinese emperor Pu Yi, age three, ascends the throne.

1911 –1912—Chinese Revolution topples the Qing dynasty and establishes a republic; Sun Yat-sen founds provisional government in Nanjing.

1919—During the May Fourth Movement, students in Beijing protest the World War I peace treaty on May 4.

1921—Chinese Communist party is formed in Shanghai by Mao Zedong and others.

1923—Sun Yat-sen forms United Front between Guomindang and the Chinese Communist party.

1925—Death of Sun Yat-sen; Chiang Kai-shek becomes commander in chief of Guomindang.

1927—Chiang Kai-shek takes over the Guomindang and moves China's capital to Nanjing; In April, the Communist party has almost fifty-eight thousand members; In spring of 1927, Chiang starts the "White Terror" and purges Communists; Mao flees to countryside.

1928—The Guomindang capture Beijing and unite China under one government.

1930—Mao establishes Communist base in the southern province of Jiangxi; Grows to one hundred twenty-two thousand members.

1931—Japan seizes China's northeast provinces.

1933—Chinese Communist party grows to three hundred thousand members.

1934 –1935—The Red Army undertakes the Long March to avoid attack by the Nationalist Army; Mao leads the way; New Communist base established in Yan'an in Jan. 1936.

1937—Japan invades China; The Communists and Guomindang join in the United Front to fight Japan.

1945—World War II ends with Japan's defeat.

1946—Truce between Guomindang and Communists is broken; Civil war resumes.

1949—Communists defeat Guomindang; On October 1, Mao announces birth of the People's Republic of China.

1950—Chinese Communist troops join North Korean Communists fighting the civil war in Korea.

1953—China's first Five-Year Plan starts; Korean War ends.

1957—Thousands of intellectuals criticize the government during the Hundred Flowers Movement; Anti-Rightist Campaign ends it in June.

1958—The Great Leap Forward is announced, setting new production goals and creating People's Communes.

1960 –1961—Massive famines sweep China.

1966—Mao launches the Cultural Revolution; *The Little Red Book* is published by Lin Biao, building the cult of Mao; Formation of Red Guards; Chaos overtakes China.

1972—U.S. president Richard Nixon meets with Mao in Beijing.

1976—Zhou Enlai dies; Deng Xiaoping is dismissed from his posts; Mao dies on September 9; On October 10, the Gang of Four is arrested.

1978—Deng Xiaoping becomes China's leader.

1979—China and the United States establish normal diplomatic relations.

1980—Gang of Four is tried and sentenced.

Chapter Notes

Chapter 1. Climbing Jiajin Mountain

1. Harrison E. Salisbury, *The Long March: The Untold Story* (New York: Harper and Row, 1985), p. 237.

2. Jonathan Spence, *Mao Zedong* (New York: Penguin, 1999), p. 83.

Chapter 2. Birth of a Rebel

1. Edgar Snow, *Red Star Over China* (New York: Grove Press, 1968), p. 132.

2. Ibid., p. 131.

3. Patricia Buckley Ebrey, *The Cambridge Illustrated History of China* (Cambridge: Cambridge University Press, 1997, p. 248.

4. Snow, p. 135.

5. Harrison E. Salisbury, *The Long March: The Untold Story* (New York: Harper & Row, 1985), p. 22.

Chapter 3. End of an Empire

1. Edgar Snow, *Red Star Over China* (New York: Grove Press, 1968), p. 142.

2. Ibid., p. 146.

3. Mao Zedong, "To The Glory of the Hans," *Selected Works of Mao Tse-tung*, Vol. 6, as viewed on *The Maoist Documentation Project*, n.d., <http://www.maoism.org/msw/vol6/mswv6_03.htm> (December 26, 2002).

4. Fredrick Engels, "The Principles of Communism," *Selected Works, Vol. 1*, Moscow, Progress Publishers, 1969, <http://www.marxists.org/archive/marx/works/1847/11/princom.htm#intro> (December 26, 2002).

5. Snow, p. 155.

6. David Remnick, "V.I. Lenin," *Time 100: Time.com*, n.d. <http://www.time.com/time/time100/leaders/profile/lenin3.html> (December 26, 2002).

Chapter 4. The Barrel of the Gun

1. Mao Zedong, "Report on Investigation of the Peasant Movement in Hunan," *Selected Works of Mao Tse tung* (Peking: Foreign Languages Press, 1967), vol. 1, pp. 23–25.

2. Mao Zedong, "Report on an Investigation of the Peasant Movement in Hunan," *Quotations from Chairman Mao Tsetung* (Peking: Foreign Languages Press, 1972), pp. 11–12.

3. Jonathan Spence, *Mao Zedong* (New York: Penguin, 1999), p. 75.

4. Edgar Snow, *Red Star Over China* (New York: Grove Press, 1968), p. 258.

5. Harrison E. Salisbury, *The Long March: The Untold Story* (New York: Harper & Row, 1985), p. 129.

6. Mao Zedong, "On Guerrilla Warfare," *Selected Works of Mao Tse-Tung, Vol. VI*, 1937, as viewed on *The Maoist Documentation Project*, n.d., <http: www.maoism.org/msw/vol6/mswv6_29.htm> (December 26, 2002).

7. Mao Zedong, "Basic Tactics," *Selected Works of Mao Tse-Tung, Vol. VI*, as viewed on *The Maoist Documentation Project*, n.d., <http://www.maoism.org/msw/vol6/mswv6_28.htm> (December 26, 2002).

Chapter 5. The People Rise Up

1. Mao Zedong, "The Long March," *China Online*, 2002, <http://chineseculture.about.com/library/literature/poetry/blsmao_el5.htm> (December 26, 2002).

2. Edgar Snow, *Red Star Over China* (New York: Harper & Row, 1985), p. 198.

3. Mao Zedong, "On Practice," *Selected Works of Mao Tse-tung, Vol. I*, as viewed on *The Maoist Documentation Project*, n.d. <http://www.maoism.org/msw/vol1/mswv1_16.htm> (December 26, 2002).

4. Mao Zedong, "On New Democracy," *Selected Works of Mao Tse-tung, Vol. II,* as viewed on *The Maoist Documentation Project,* n.d., <http://www.maoism.org/msw/vol2/mswv2_26.htm> (December 26, 2002).

Chapter 6. A New China

1. Mao Zedong, "The Chinese People Have Stood Up!" *Selected Works of Mao Tse-Tung, Vol. V,* as viewed on *The Maoist Documentation Project,* n.d., <http://www.maoism.org/msw/vol5/mswv5_01.htm> (December 26, 2002).

2. Dr. Li Zhi Sui, *The Private Life of Chairman Mao* (New York: Random House, 1994), p. 52.

3. Jonathan Spence, *Mao Zedong* (New York, Penguin, 1999), p. 118.

4. Mao Zedong, "On the Draft Constitution of the People's Republic of China," *Selected Works of Mao Tse-tung, Vol. V,* as viewed on *The Maoist Documentation Project,* n.d., <http://www.maoism.org/msw/vol5/mswv5_37.htm> (December 26, 2002).

5. Mao Zedong, "On The Co-operative Transformation of Agriculture," *Selected Works of Mao Tse-tung, Vol. V,* as viewed on *The Maoist Documentation Project,* n.d., <http://www.maoism.org/msw/vol5/mswv5_44.htm> (December 26, 2002).

6. "Preamble And Excerpts From The Constitution Of The People's Republic Of China ("PRC")," *Electric Law Library,* <http://www.lectlaw.com/files/int11.htm> (December 26, 2002).

7. Ibid.

8. Mao Zedong, Introduction note to "Women Have Gone to the Labour Front," *Quotations from Chairman Mao Tsetung,* (Peking: Foreign Languages Press, 1967), p. 297.

Chapter 7. Trouble and Turmoil

1. Jonathan Spence, *Mao Zedong,* (New York: Penguin, 1999), p. 131.

2. Ibid.

3. Rose Tang, "Revolution's Children: The collapse of ideology leaves generations adrift in a moral vacuum," *Asiaweek*, September 24, 1999, <http://image. pathfinder.com:81/http:/www.asiaweek.com/asiaweek/ magazine/99/0924/cn_journeys.html> (December 26, 2002).

4. Ibid.

5. Mao Zedong, "The Masses Can Do Anything," *Selected Works of Mao Tse-tung, Vol. VIII*, as viewed on *The Maoist Documentaion Project*, <http://www.maoism.org/ msw/vol8/mswv8_16.htm>.

6. Ross Terrill, *China in Our Time* (New York: Simon and Schuster, 1992), p. 33.

Chapter 8. The Cultural Revolution

1. Philip Short, *Mao: A Life* (New York: Henry Holt and Company, 1999), p. 541.

2. Liang Heng and Judith Shapiro, *Son of the Revolution* (New York: Vintage Books, 1984), p. 68.

3. Jung Chang, *Wild Swans: Three Daughters of China* (New York: Simon and Schuster, 1991), p. 304.

4. Short, p. 543.

5. Jonathan Spence, *Mao Zedong*, (New York, Penguin, 1999), p. 164.

6. Nien Cheng, *Life and Death in Shanghai* (New York: Grove Press, 1986), p. 274.

7. "Chinese National Anthem," n.d. <http:// www.geocities.com/Tokyo/Temple/2654/china_historic/prc. htm> (December 26, 2002).

8. Hugh Sidey, "Excursions in Mao's China," *Time*, March 6, 1972, p. 17.

9. Dr. Li Rhi Sui, *The Private Life of Chairman Mao* (New York: Random House, 1994), p. 86.

10. Anchee Min, *Red Azalea* (New York: Berkley Books, 1994), p. 17.

11. "Nixon's China Odyssey," *Time*, March 6, 1972, p. 14.

12. Chang, p. 292.

13. Ibid.

Chapter 9. Opening the Doors

1. Richard Nixon, *The Memoirs of Richard Nixon* (New York: Simon & Schuster, 1978), p. 553.

2. "Nixon's China Game, The American Experience," *PBS*, 1999, <http://www.pbs.org/wgbh/amex/china/peopleevents/pande01.html> (May, 2002).

3. "Nixon's China Game."

4. Henry Kissinger, *Years of Renewal* (New York: Simon and Schuster, 1999), p. 142.

5. "Shanghai Communique," *The New York Times Archive*, February 28, 1972, <http:www.nytimes.com/library/world/asia/022872us-china-text.html> (May 2002).

6. "Nixon's China Odyssey," *Time*, March 6, 1972, p. 16.

7. Reuters, "Mao Tse-Tung Dies in Peking at 82," *The New York Times*, September 10, 1976, p. 1.

8. Anchee Min, *Red Azalea* (New York: Berkley Books, 1994), p. 327.

Chapter 10. The Legacy of Mao's Revolution

1. *The Heart of the Dragon: Remembering*, A.S.H. Films, 1984.

2. Quoted by Immanuel C. Y. Hsü, *China Without Mao: The Search for a New Order* (Oxford: Oxford University Press, 1982), p. 151.

3. Quoted by George J. Church, "Deng Xiaoping," *Time*, January 6, 1986, <http://www.time.com/time/special/moy/1985.html> (December 26, 2002).

4. Hsü, p. 150.

5. Ross Terrill, "China, the Uncertain Ally," *The New York Times,* Feb. 19, 2002, p. A23.

Further Reading and Internet Addresses

Books

Allan, Tony. *The Making of Modern China*. Chicago: Heinemann Library, 2002.

Chen, Da. *China's Son: Growing Up in the Cultural Revolution*. New York: Delacorte Press, 2001.

Field, Catherine. *China*. Austin, New York: Raintree Steck-Vaughn Publishers, 2000.

Hatt, Christine. *Mao Zedong*. Milwaukee: World Almanac Library, 2003.

Jiang, Ji-Li. *Red Scarf Girl: A Memoir of the Cultural Revolution*. New York: HarperCollins, 1997.

Slavicek, Louise Chipley, *Mao Zedong*. Philadelphia: Chelsea House Publishers, 2003.

Internet Addresses

"About China." *Embassy of the People's Republic of China in the United States of America*. n.d. <www.china-embassy.org/eng/c2685.html>.

China—A Country Study. n.d. <http://lcweb2.loc.gov/frd/cs/cntoc.html>.

The Mao Zedong Reference Archive. n.d. <www.marxists.org/reference/archive/mao/>.

126

Index